Coping

WITH COLLEGE

A GUIDE FOR ACADEMIC SUCCESS

THIRD EDITION

Alice L. Hamachek

CENTRAL MICHIGAN UNIVERSITY

D0023946

PEARSON

Prentice
Hall

Upper Saddle River, New Jersey
Columbus, Ohio

Library of Congress Cataloging in Publication Data
Hamachek, Alice L.
    Coping with college : a guide for academic success / Alice L. Hamachek.—3rd ed.
        p.   cm.
    Includes bibliographical references and index.
    ISBN 0-13-170692-6
    1. College student orientation—Handbooks, manuals, etc.   2. Study
    skills—Handbooks, manuals, etc.   3. Motivation in education—Handbooks,
    manuals, etc.   I. Title
LB2343.3.H36   2007
378.1'98—dc22   2005037486

Vice President and Executive Publisher: Jeffery W. Johnston
Executive Editor: Sande Johnson
Developmental Editor: Jennifer Gessner
Editorial Assistant: Susan Kauffman
Production Editor: Alexandrina Benedicto Wolf
Production Coordinator: Holcomb Hathaway
Design Coordinator: Diane C. Lorenzo
Cover Designer: Kristina D. Holmes
Cover Image: Images.com
Production Manager: Pamela D. Bennet
Director of Marketing: Dave Gesell
Marketing Manager: Amy Judd

This book was set in Goudy by Integra. It was printed and bound by
R. R. Donnelley & Sons Company. The cover was printed by Phoenix Color Corp.

Pearson Education Ltd.   Pearson Education Australia Pty. Limited
Pearson Education Singapore Pte. Ltd.   Pearson Education North Asia Ltd.
Pearson Education Canada, Ltd.   Pearson Educación de Mexico, S.A. de C.V.
Pearson Education—Japan   Pearson Education Malaysia Pte. Ltd.

10 9 8 7 6 5 4 3 2

ISBN 0-13-170692-6

Dedication

To all the visionaries who desire
to leave a legacy of learning
etched in excellence!

Contents

MOTIVATION   21

GOAL SETTING   29

TIME MANAGEMENT   35

PROCRASTINATION   47

MEMORY TECHNIQUES   111

VOCABULARY ENHANCEMENT   123

TESTING GUIDELINES   137

Preface

Coping with College: A Guide for Academic Success is a great book for anyone interested in achieving academic excellence in educational endeavors. The book is filled with practical suggestions for the action-oriented student who functions in a fast-paced world that values excellence. It contains key elements that form the foundational framework for attaining outstanding achievement in higher-level academic settings.

The style of the writing is informal, and the tone is friendly. The information in this book can easily be applied to various learning situations. The approach to learning is positive and suggests that studying can be an enjoyable experience when success is likely.

Clinical and classroom settings provided the background experiences for this book. Research for the content was conducted over a period of years and included interviews with many students throughout the United States. Therefore, suggestions in this book represent the knowledge of years of study, the wisdom of years of teaching, and the advice of students who were actually encountering the daily challenges of college life.

Each chapter is written so it can be used independently or blended with other chapters to form an integrated whole. The independent nature of each chapter allows the student to target particular areas and get needed information without reading the entire text. The text is organized to make specific information readily accessible so it can be instantly applied.

Coping with College encourages the student to become actively involved in the content and apply the skills and strategies for academic success. It gives the student direct instruction related to the topics presented, as well as guidelines for enhancing one's depth of knowledge and understanding. Therefore, the student can do as little or as much as necessary to accomplish the desired outcome.

This third edition of *Coping with College* has been revised, rewritten, and reorganized. Two new chapters, titled "Critical Thinking" and "Listening," have been added. Major sections related to classroom etiquette, getting the most from your education, and improving your reading speed and comprehension also have been added, as well as two practical models related to goal setting and writing a paper. The sequence of chapters and the organization within individual chapters have been adjusted to incorporate the new segments and to enhance the flow and presentation of the text. Readers will find that the new vocabulary illustrations, drawings, and cartoons offer an amusing dimension to the book.

A significant change to this edition is the inclusion of Enrichment Activities at the end of each chapter. These diverse activities provide opportunities for independent use by the student or classroom use by the professor. The flexibility of the activities will accommodate personal style, creativity, and dualistic purposes.

It has been said that *success is a journey*. Thus, if academic triumph and good fortune occur frequently, the journey, though it may be long and difficult, will be more enjoyable! Believe in yourself! Believe in your dreams! Accept the challenge and claim the victory!

ACKNOWLEDGMENTS

I would like to thank the following reviewers for their helpful comments: Jacek Dalecki, Indiana University; Anthony Easley, Valencia Community College, FL; Peter Haverkos, Miami University, OH; Starletta Barber Poindexter, Normandale Community College, MN; Mary Silva, Modesto Junior College, CA; and Loraine Woods, Jackson State University, MS.

Matriculation!

ongratulations!
You have met all the requirements to be matriculated at the university!

1. Start packing!
2. Call your friends!
3. Buy an organizer!
4. Get a phone card!
5. Take your checkbook!
6. Leave the video games at home!
7. Sell your high school jersey!
8. Pay your tuition!
9. Clean your room!
10. Ready, set, go!

College

THE DEMANDS OF COLLEGE

The demands of college are significantly different from those of high school. The academic curriculum, the rigors of academic expectations and evaluations, the available resources, and your particular course of study and performance in high school are all factors that will play a part in determining the challenge of the transition from high school to college.

Also, going from a small high school to a large university may be difficult. The larger the university, the more complex the organizational and physical structure, which will put additional strains on your organizational, spatial, and social skills.

Although the specific differences between high school and college will vary depending on your particular situation, the following sections will alert you to some major considerations that will likely affect your transition and adjustment. Some of the problems and pitfalls are outlined to help you cope with them before they conquer you.

1. Living Environment

One of your first college challenges will be learning to enjoy your new living environment. At college, you will likely live in a residence hall on campus, in a sorority or fraternity house, or in a private apartment. Some colleges require new students to live on campus during their first one or two years of university life. Whatever your situation, you will probably have less privacy and less space than you had at home and will find yourself adjusting to roommates with personalities and preferences different from yours.

Finding compatible roommates is significant, because roommates will profoundly affect your emotional and social state. Work hard to make good choices in establishing roommate relationships. However, if you have difficulty, be sure to consult the appropriate supervisor for assistance. Once you feel good about your living situation and have a harmonious relationship with your roommates, you will be free to focus your attention on your academic goals.

You will likely be free to arrange and decorate your living area. Designing a pleasant living environment will be a cooperative effort among the one or more persons with whom you reside. It is important to personalize your designated living space. However, resist the temptation to make it so cozy and comfortable that you emphasize the social aspects of university life more than your academic studies.

2. Independence

For some students, the college experience will be their first real taste of independence. Independence can be a joy, but it also requires a considerable amount of discipline and accountability. On a daily basis, you will be making major decisions regarding time, activities, relationships, and academic study. Also, you will make minor decisions about eating, recreation, staying out late, and getting to class. Choices have outcomes. Wise choices usually enhance your life and reputation, while immature decisions more likely result in difficulties such as academic probation, conflict in relationships, and diminished opportunities. The pace of college life moves quickly. You will be surprised how rapidly the weeks of the semester or term roll by. Therefore, using your independence to "do your own thing" may not be the best choice, particularly if your behavior does not coincide with the expectations of academic excellence.

Independence is wonderful; however, don't forget it requires a great deal of responsibility! Don't get caught off guard. If you get behind, it is *hard to get caught up!* Balance independence and accountability wisely. You won't be sorry.

3. Size of the College Campus

The size of the college campus can be intimidating. Whereas the traditional high school may consist of a single building, a university campus may span hundreds of acres. The familiarity of one building must be exchanged for many buildings that may be far apart, look quite similar, and have a number of levels and intricate floor plans.

If you have spatial, directional, or orientation difficulties, you may experience some problems. It may be difficult for you to organize your schedule to be able to get from one class to another in the time allotted for class transition. You may find yourself late for classes because you end up in the wrong building or room. You may get to your classroom and discover that the location has been changed and you don't know how to find the new location.

4. Class Size

In college, some classes may have more than 100 students enrolled. Often, these classes are held in large lecture halls or auditoriums. Students may not have seat assignments; thus, you may never be seated next to the same person throughout the term. It may be difficult to get to know individuals well enough to feel comfortable studying with them or consulting them if you have questions or concerns.

Some large classes may be taught by a person, or the instruction may be done via television, video, or other forms of educational technology. If a large class is taught by a person, it may be one professor, several professors, or a team consisting of a professor and graduate assistants. Consequently, you may find it more difficult to establish a relationship with your instructor or have the instructor know you by name and face.

Large-class formats may make it difficult to see the visual aids and hear the lecture. You may not have a choice of seating location and may find yourself at the back of the room, with no chance to relocate.

Also, it may be much harder for you to concentrate since there will be many distractions. With large groups, there likely will be more movement, more coughing, more talking, and even more "goofing off"! Because college professors don't expect to have to enforce discipline, some students may take this opportunity to socialize and consequently cause you to be distracted from the task at hand.

5. Schedule of Daily Classes

In college, the daily schedule of classes is more diverse than it was in high school. In high school, the daily schedule was probably the same almost every day. In college, classes are structured differently. For example, you may have some classes that meet for one hour on Monday, Wednesday, and Friday, others that meet for 90 minutes on Tuesday and Thursday, and a night class that meets for three hours on a single day. Interspersed may be a lab session that meets periodically. Thus, your daily schedule may be very different from the one you experienced in high school.

Your concentration and ability to stay on task may be taxed to the limit in the longer class sessions and on days when you have more hours of classes. In addition, your class schedule will change completely as semesters or terms end and begin, and you will have to readjust to different classes and a new time frame.

This less-structured hourly schedule may create problems for the student who is not aware of the pitfalls. Since you will not have classes scheduled every hour on the hour, you should use some of that unscheduled time to study. Consequently, it will be important that you program your day with classes and study periods. Don't be tricked into believing that, since you have attended your class sessions, you don't have anything else to do.

CHOOSING CLASSES

R egistration is a time for students to select the courses they need to meet such academic requirements as majors, minors, curricula, certificates, and specific degrees. A good schedule with appropriate classes can be vital to your academic success in any one term or semester. Therefore, it is important that you spend time and energy planning before you make final selections.

Following are some considerations to help you in making appropriate course selections.

1. Seek advice from a counselor, an academic advisor, or a professor to discuss the classes that might best "fit together."

2. Ask other students for information about specific classes and professors, but remember that students' opinions may not accurately reflect the quality of a class. Not all students have the same learning styles or the same learning needs. A class that was unsatisfactory for someone else may be very good for you. Thus, be sure you seek information rather than just opinions.

"Dad, I've decided to change my major."

3. Go to the bookstore and review the textbooks that are required for a particular class or section. Look at the length of the textbook and the size of the print. Evaluate the readability of the text and determine the quality of its organization. Look for useful reference aids, such as glossaries and appendices.

4. Visit with the professor! Inquire about the professor's style and methodology as well as her attitude toward students who have learning disabilities or who need extra assistance. Ask about the reading requirements, the graded paper or project requirements, and additional out-of-class assignments. Also, find out about building location, hour of class, seating arrangements, and how the grading system works. These factors may be significant to your academic success.

5. Space out your classes so you will not be rushed and will have time to review before and after class. Think about organizing your classes so you won't be wasting a lot of time walking back and forth between buildings or traveling from one side of campus to the other.

6. Choose class times that are compatible with your biological clock. For example, if you are not a morning person, it may not be wise for you to take an early class. Try to use the best part of your day to take the classes that require the most concentration.

CLASSROOM ETIQUETTE

he college community is a subset of the larger society and is made up of people who have many cultural, lifestyle, personality, character, and economic differences. Thus, when a group of these individuals gather together in a given room as professors and classmates, they will have a variety of preferences related to values and the way each likes to function.

Social courtesies are important in all social situations. In the classroom, they can contribute to better interpersonal relationships and an environment that will be more conducive to learning. In conversations with professors and students, the following five issues have surfaced and, therefore, will be used to stimulate thought and discussion.

1. Talking and passing notes during class instruction interferes with others' ability to hear and concentrate. Many classes are large, and the professor and students may not have opportunities for direct eye contact. You may be tempted to chitchat and conduct other activities, as the professor will likely be unaware of your inattention. Thus, it is your responsibility to be aware of those around you who want to benefit from the information presented and curb your disruptive behaviors until class has ended.

2. Cell phones are wonderful, but, when used without appropriate courtesies in regards to others, they can be irritating and disruptive. It is good classroom etiquette to turn off pagers and cell phones when class is in session. Some professors will make this mandatory by noting it on the syllabus. Others will expect that you are savvy enough to recognize that it is inappropriate to take calls during class, and getting up to leave the classroom may give the message that class is not that important.

3. Baseball caps have become popular for both men and women. Social etiquette indicates that hats should be removed in specific situations, but that formality has taken on a casual compliance in recent years. If, however, you are fortunate enough to have a professor who wants to have eye contact during lectures and personal interactions, then removing your hat or tipping it back to clearly reveal your face will make that more likely. Be sensitive to your professor's preferences and remember that mutual respect and courteous behaviors rarely go unnoticed.

4. Personal habits that are oblivious to one person may be annoying to another. A list of common bothersome habits in the classroom would likely include the following: snapping gum, tapping pencils, cracking knuckles, rustling a newspaper, snoring, and making weird noises. Stop for a moment and think of some things that annoy you when you are trying to concentrate. Make an effort to monitor any behaviors that interrupt full attention to class instruction.

off the mark   by Mark Parisi
w w w . o f f t h e m a r k . c o m

MAYBE ONE OF THE REASONS YOUR FRIENDS TREAT YOU WITH SUCH DISRESPECT IS THE FACT YOU'VE NEVER CHANGED YOUR SHIRT...

offthemark.com   ATLANTIC FEATURE © 1996 MARK PARISI

5. A discussion of personal hygiene can be difficult because it is usually a sensitive subject. However, poor personal hygiene can be an irritant when people are in close proximity within group situations. Take inventory of your appearance, clothing, breath, and any negative odors. Modify those you can, and you will discover that your social acceptance will be greatly improved.

BECOMING A MORE EFFECTIVE STUDENT

Your job in college is to be a student. You will want to be a good one!

The goal of all educational instruction is learning. Learning is commonly defined as a change of behavior. You likely have learned how to tie your shoes, write your name, and drive a car. These were things that at one time you did not know how to do. However, you learned and, thus, your behavior changed. You now know how to do those things.

For the most part, the challenge isn't learning itself. You have great ability to learn, or you wouldn't have made it to college. More likely, academic problems occur when your learning isn't efficient or effective.

How do you become a more efficient and effective student? Here are some general principles. Mastering them will be among the most important academic accomplishments that you will ever achieve.

1. Make a Commitment to Excellence

Study to become a more educated individual. Keep long-range goals in mind so you won't be tempted to study just to pass the exam! Make knowledge, accuracy, and promptness key attributes of all your assignments. Remember, you are not "just getting through college"; you are developing your selfhood and forming the foundation of your academic knowledge for a lifetime.

2. Understand Your Learning Style

Each person is unique and has a learning style that has evolved by natural development, personal preference, and mandatory accommodations. Although there are many ways to accomplish a desired result, as you understand and acknowledge the style that works best for you, you will spend less time using nonproductive efforts. Keep in mind, however, that the college years offer opportunities for exploration. So, be willing to be flexible and incorporate new perspectives as you continue to advance your personal and professional self.

3. Acquire a Wide Range of Learning Strategies

Good students have access to many learning strategies and have learned when, where, and how to use each strategy to best accomplish the desired learning goals. Learn as many study and memory strategies as you can. Be willing to try new strategies that you haven't tried before. Remember that what worked before may not be what will work best now. Explore new options and continue to challenge yourself to study with greater efficiency.

4. Spend Time Studying

Many students think that they are spending lots of time studying. However, study time includes only the time you spend focused on the task. It does not include the time you spend getting organized, daydreaming, or tuning into distractions.

Time is one of your most important learning resources because it is directly under your control. Each day has 24 fixed hours. You cannot add hours to your day. You can only make effective use of the time you have.

Research makes it quite clear that no substitute exists for the amount of time spent studying. An increase in study time strongly relates to an increase in learning. This principle is one of the most important you will ever learn. If effectively applied to your studies, it will be invaluable in your quest to be a successful student.

5. Develop Self-Discipline

You are in a stage of development that allows you more freedom and independence than you perhaps have ever had before. Most students look forward to this stage. However, with independence comes responsibility.

College is different from high school in many respects. One difference is the greater need to discipline yourself. At its root, the term *discipline* means "guidance" or "leading." You will find many people who are willing to help you, but you must take the initiative. You will need to lead yourself through an analysis of your own study habits, determine your strengths and your deficiencies, and seek guidance in making yourself a more effective learner. Remember the adage: If it's going to be, it's up to me!

6. Recognize the Opportunities of University Life

University life offers wonderful opportunities for developing character, expanding knowledge, and experiencing a dimension of society that will never again have quite the same composition. A significant part of becoming an effective student is knowing what resources are available and how to access them. Unfortunately, many students neglect to use the numerous physical and intellectual resources offered by the university. Your college years are your prime learning years. Don't miss the opportunity to take advantage of the wealth of knowledge at your fingertips.

NONTRADITIONAL STUDENTS

raditionally, college-bound students have graduated from high school and immediately entered programs of higher education in preparation for a lifelong career. During recent years, however, the status quo has shifted in relation to the age, gender, and purpose of many college students. For example, some women may have put off going to college until after they raised a family, and they are now attending college at a slightly older age than the traditional college student. Also, for a variety of reasons, some individuals are returning to college to pursue a second degree in preparation for a career change. These factors, along with others, have contributed to a shift in the average age, experience, and purpose of the college population.

A common reference term used to describe students of this nature is *nontraditional*. Nontraditional students have unique challenges that likely will not affect traditional students. Some of these challenges include having responsibilities of children and family life, commuting long distances, taking night classes, and being disconnected from the daily routine of studying.

The academic suggestions given throughout this book are relevant for nontraditional as well as traditional students. However, making time for studying while caring for children requires some additional creative thought. The following suggestions can assist in this process.

1. Create projects your children can do while you are studying.
2. Include your children in your study and learning activities because they often enjoy being helpers.
3. Take breaks to be with your children; they may be more willing to spend time alone if they have had time with you.
4. Specify "do-not-interrupt" times for intense study.
5. Employ playmates, neighbors, and relatives to care for your children during crucial study periods.
6. Occupy children's attention with appropriate long-play DVDs or videos during study times.
7. Establish a block of study time for you and your children to complete homework.

8. Prepare a weekly schedule so your family will have advance knowledge of your study plan.

9. Be firm about bedtime routines so you can plan on a given amount of study time.

10. Remember that your family is more important than your studies, but with proper planning you can have success with both.

WHY AM I ATTENDING COLLEGE?

 person chooses to attend college for many reasons. Some of them might be considered "good" reasons, while others might be considered "bad" reasons. Regardless, the commitment you make to being a successful college student will likely be reflected in the reasons behind your decision to attend college.

Use the following list to stimulate your thinking and help you focus on your feelings and your purpose for being in college. If your purpose or feeling is not included, add it to the list.

COLLEGE IS:

1. a place to party!
2. an avenue for career development.
3. an opportunity to get away from home.
4. a possibility to develop more of my potential.
5. a chance to participate in athletics.
6. the best hope for obtaining the kind of life I desire.
7. an alternative to getting a job or going into the military service.
8. what my parents want for me.
9. what I want for myself.
10. the fulfillment of a dream.
11. the freedom to begin again.
12. a place to find a mate.
13. an escape.

Once you have specified your main reason for attending college, think about its compatibility with intensive academic study. If your reason is not compatible, you may need to prepare yourself for difficulties when report card time comes. Getting a good college education requires a commitment to academic excellence. In college, studying is a full-time job. Remember, it's tougher to catch up than it is to keep up!

Enrichment Activities

1. What is your primary purpose for attending college? Specify some details of that purpose. What are some secondary purposes?

2. Explain your greatest concern about the college experience.

3. List some of your deficiencies and efficiencies as a student.

4. What are you specifically doing to commit to excellence in academic accomplishments?

5. Research some of the academic resources and job opportunities available to you at your college.

6. What observations have you made in relationship to your ability to practice self-discipline?

7. Compare and contrast the needs and challenges of traditional and nontraditional students. How can each group assist the other?

2

Professors

As a student, you will have a special relationship with each of your professors. This does not necessarily mean that it will be personal or wonderful. Rather, it means that it will be one that requires good working dynamics of the same nature as those in best-friend interactions.

Professors are people, too, and if you learn and use the skills that create good friendships, you will have a distinct advantage when you interact with your professors.

Following are some important principles to help you with your relationships with professors.

ATTEND CLASS REGULARLY

If you are registered for a class, the professor expects you to attend. Be there!

Some students make the mistake of thinking that they do not have to attend class if they don't want to. Their reasoning is that, since they are paying tuition to take the class, they can determine whether or not they attend. This is immature thinking.

Attend class regularly and, if possible, arrive early. Use this time to talk with the professor or your fellow classmates. If you don't care to

13

interact, review your notes or just relax. Your attendance and lack of tardiness will help demonstrate your commitment to excellence.

If you are still not convinced that you should attend class regularly, check the policy on attendance recorded in your university bulletin. Often, unknown to students, the professor "is authorized to lower scholastic ratings if the student's absences or latenesses require this action" (Central Michigan University, 2000, p. 68).

BE ATTENTIVE

ost professors practice good eye contact with their students, so it is important that you are attentive in class. Sleeping, day-dreaming, or doing such activities as writing letters are inappropriate behaviors for the serious student.

Even more inappropriate is talking with your neighbor while the professor is speaking. This personally insults the instructor and also disturbs the other students. Besides, you will miss what is being said, which may be vital information. The temptation to talk is often great, but make it a practice to avoid doing this.

PARTICIPATE IN CLASS DISCUSSIONS AND ACTIVITIES

ike good friendships, teaching and learning are two-way streets. Teachers are expected to teach, and learners are expected to learn. You will have a better chance of learning if you partici-pate actively in class discussions and activities.

You may have become conditioned over the years to interact infre-quently during class discussions. This lack of interaction will not do! You must change!

Often, students do not ask questions or volunteer to answer those that are asked. This gives the impression that they either do not know the answers or aren't willing to participate—both negative impressions.

Participating in class gives the impression that you are prepared and interested in advancing your own knowledge. Just as you remember those with whom you converse more often, professors, too, remember those who participate, due to the more frequent one-to-one interaction. Thus, they are more likely to make a greater investment in developing that special student–teacher bond. Asking questions or making comments just to be noticed, however, wastes class time and often has a negative impact.

CULTIVATE A POSITIVE ATTITUDE TOWARD CLASS

 our attitude can make or break your performance in a class. You may hear conflicting opinions from other students about professors. But, remember that these are just opinions. A bad teacher for another student may be the best teacher for you. We all learn differently and have personality preferences. Decide for yourself.

Evaluate your attitude toward the class and professor. Understand full well that your performance can be affected by your attitude. Whether the class or professor is good or bad may be irrelevant. What you learn and what you contribute in class may reflect your attitude more than the class or professor. Besides, a professor may not change to meet your preferences, so, ultimately, it will be up to you to take charge.

HELP THE PROFESSOR KNOW YOU BY NAME

 ue to the very nature of college, many classes are large and impersonal. A number of your classes will be lectures held in large classrooms or lecture halls.

Professors do not have much opportunity to know who you are unless you take the initiative. Do it! Make opportunities to interact with your professor in a formal or informal manner. The interaction doesn't have to be long or complex, so don't be intimidated by your lack of confidence in knowing what to do or say. Keep it simple, but genuine.

Early in the semester or term, make an appointment to meet

"The eggheads have landed!"

personally and privately with your professor. Many professors have designated office hours for the purpose of interacting with students. Most are delighted to talk to students since this is an integral part of their chosen profession. However, since professors are busy people, make your visit brief. Indicate that your purpose is to introduce yourself. Share some personal goals or concerns you have in relationship to the class. Be sincere. You won't be sorry.

LEARN THE PROFESSOR'S LIKES AND DISLIKES

 rofessors are human and have likes and dislikes just as you do. It's understood that dislikes offer greater opportunities for irritations and negative impressions. On the other hand, likes open the door for harmony and positive interactions. So, it seems wise to listen to the professor's comments about likes and dislikes and attempt to be in harmony with the positive preferences. You may want to read or reread Dale Carnegie's classic book, *How to Win Friends and Influence People* (1936).

ARRANGE CONFERENCES BEFORE IT'S TOO LATE

conference with your professor may be necessary if difficulties or differences arise. Also, additional clarification or input may be needed. Don't wait until the end is near or you're in deep trouble before you seek additional assistance. Seek help early.

Make an appointment. Don't try to solve a problem in the hurried moments before or after class. It may be inappropriate or uncomfortable to deal with a problem in the presence of other students.

If you are meeting with your professor to discuss some differences, don't begin with a personal attack on the professor. Judgments of this nature limit the potential for open and effective communication. Remember, it is the teacher's role to judge and evaluate.

Express your complaint in terms of the specific problem rather than a personal attack. For example, the statement "This paper took a lot of time and you gave me a C" could be better presented by saying "I worked hard on this paper and was disappointed that I didn't get a B." Watch your use of "I" and "you" messages because "you" messages often place blame.

Listen to your professor's comments, and be willing to discuss your questions and concerns. Ask for what you want. Don't expect your professor to know your wishes. Work for resolution, and be willing to negotiate your differences, redo your assignment, or suggest other solutions that you think would be appropriate.

If you are not satisfied with the resolution of the meeting, you have several options. One is to let it go. Another is to talk to the person at the next level of power, who often will be the department chairperson. If you still are dissatisfied and feel you have a just concern, go to the next higher level. If your concern involves a grade, a policy and procedure governing grade grievances usually exists.

LEARN FROM YOUR PROFESSORS

 rofessors are an integral part of your education. They have much to teach you, so learn from them. Unless you know it all, there is always something more for you to learn. Respect their knowledge even if you don't like them personally or their system of delivery. Learning from the negative can be just as valuable as learning from the positive.

Be a good consumer of the educational opportunities that college offers. Professors will come and go in your life, but your education will be with you forever!

WHEN PROFESSORS TALK FAST

 ates of speaking vary. Some people speak fast, and others speak slowly. Whatever the rate, you hope that your listening pace is about the same as the professor's speaking pace. Of course, if you are taking notes, this means that you will need to listen and write as fast as the professor is speaking. If you can do this, then there is no problem. If you can't keep up, however, here are some suggestions.

1. Ask permission to tape-record the lecture. However, tape only the information that you want to listen to a second time. Remember, if you tape for an hour, then you must reserve an hour to listen to the tape. Use the pause or stop button to eliminate the speaking that you don't need to record.

2. Be willing to ask the professor to repeat information. Also, you might ask the professor to use graphics or visual aids to help you get the information that you may miss from the spoken presentation.

3. Exchange photocopies of class notes with your classmates. It may be wise to look at notes from two different classmates. Each student may perceive the information differently and have unique ways of recording it.

4. Be familiar with the subject matter of the lecture. Make an effort to get acquainted with the content to be discussed so you will be in a better position to pick out the key points. The more you know about a subject in advance, the less you will have to focus on each and every word that is spoken.

5. Focus on key points. Don't try to write everything down. If you get behind, leave a big space in your notes. Try to stay with the lecture. Otherwise, you may mix up the information you've already heard because you are writing about something quite different from what you are now hearing.

6. Leave large empty spaces in your notes if you think you are missing chunks of information because the professor is presenting the information faster than you can record it. Use some type of symbol at this point in your notes to alert you that you missed some information.

7. Use more abbreviations than you might normally use. Set aside a time right after class to write the complete words and fill in any missing points that you remember being discussed.

8. Be sure to sit in a position in the classroom that will enable good hearing. You may be missing information because the professor is speaking fast, but the problem will be compounded if you can't hear well.

9. If you missed some information, you have several choices. One is to ask one of your peers to assist you. Another is to take your notes to the professor and ask for help with the missing chunks of information.

10. Be willing to discuss your needs with the professor. Professors are more than willing to help when asked.

11. Don't panic! You are smart enough to figure out a way to get the information that you need. Be resourceful.

On Your Own

Make a list of other strategies you can use to help you when professors talk too fast for you to understand. Ask other students what they do in this situation.

_____

_____

_____

_____

Enrichment Activities

1. Organize teams to debate the position that "professors are authorized to lower a grade if a student's absence or tardiness warrant such action."
2. Convince the professor that it is or is not important to participate in class interactive activities.
3. Role-play a student and a professor having a conference related to a failing grade on a term paper or an examination.
4. Analyze your attitude toward each of your classes. Keep track of how your attitude affects your classroom and academic performance.
5. Ask five professors to tell you about their "pet peeves" or annoyances with student behavior.

3

Motivation

ON THE ROAD TO SUCCESS

Success is a journey. Sometimes the journey will be easy, and sometimes it will be hard. When you encounter bumps and barriers, inspiration and motivation will help you stay on the right path. If you get overwhelmed and the world seems a little dark, read and reflect on these words of wisdom and enjoy a triumphant journey.

1. Believe! You must believe. Believe in yourself, believe in others, and believe in the process of life. You are here for a purpose, and you are the only one who can do what you have been called on to do.

2. Keep an open mind! Be aware of the things that are working and the things that are not. Be willing to change the latter. Be open to new methods and new experiences. Resistance to change limits possibilities.

3. Recognize when you need help, and be willing to ask for it! You will find many people willing to assist you if they know what you need. Be specific with your request.

4. Develop an attitude of gratitude! Be grateful for what you have and have been given. Be grateful for what is going to come into your life, trusting that it will be good.

5. Use your resources! Many resources are available to you. Profit from them: people, books, nature, life experiences, travel, and technology—that which is seen and that which is unseen.

6. Remember that storms never last! The sun will shine again. Clouds are temporary. Forever know that behind the clouds, the sun is always shining.

7. Celebrate who you are and why you are here! Remind yourself of what is to be accomplished. Keep your eyes on your goals. Always look to the future; keep your chin up, your feet marching forward, and your energy directed toward your life's ambition.

8. Balance your life! When things aren't in balance, they wobble, creating a wear and tear on a part of your life force. A weariness occurs when life's energies are out of harmony. Body, mind, and spirit need nurturing on a daily basis. If you neglect one, you will be in danger of draining the life energy from another. Soon, you will have two that are in deficit. Maintain a healthy equilibrium.

9. Enjoy the day! Life is short and tomorrow is an unknown, so seize each hour that has been given to you. You are important; no one else can do exactly what you can do or be exactly who you are.

10. Go for it! You have all the time, talent, and tools necessary to succeed. Be willing to risk. Be willing to fail. Be willing to succeed. *All* experiences in life are great teachers. If we are willing, we learn great lessons from everything. We gain character and strength from all of life's events, both positive and negative. Trust the process. Trust the powers that are yours to use. Smile! Laugh! Cry! *The victory is yours! You are a winner!*

Frank and Ernest

©2003 by Thaves. Reprinted with permission.

BE WILLING TO TRY AND TRY AND TRY!

he prerequisite for mastery in most activities is the willingness to try and try the activity over and over again. More often than not, you will need to try, fail, correct your errors, try again, and perhaps fail again. The key is that you keep trying!

Success doesn't come easily for most people. To become good at something often takes lots of hard work and many attempts.

Consider the poem below, which speaks of the struggles of humankind. The poem's message is valuable, and you may need to read the poem often.

> Don't Quit
>
> When things go wrong, as they sometimes will,
> When the road you're trudging seems all up hill,
> When the funds are low and the debts are high,
> And you want to smile, but you have to sigh,
> When care is pressing you down a bit,
> Rest, if you must—but don't you quit.
>
> Life is queer with its twists and turns,
> As everyone of us sometimes learns,
> And many a failure turns about
> When he might have won had he stuck it out;
> Don't give up, though the pace seems slow—
> You might succeed with another blow.
>
> Often the goal is nearer than
> It seems to a faint and faltering man,
> Often the struggler has given up
> When he might have captured the victor's cup.
> And he learned too late, when the night slipped down,
> How close he was to the golden crown.
>
> Success is failure turned inside out—
> The silver tint of the clouds of doubt—
> And you never can tell how close you are,
> It may be near when it seems afar;
> So stick to the fight when you're hardest hit—
> It's when things seem worst that you mustn't quit.
>
> —Anonymous

Some people keep going, even when they fail again and again. Consider the failures of the following politician:

1.	Failed in business	1831
2.	Defeated for legislature	1832
3.	Second failure in business	1833
4.	Suffered nervous breakdown	1836
5.	Defeated for speaker	1840
6.	Defeated for elector	1840
7.	Defeated for Congress	1843
8.	Defeated for Senate	1855
9.	Defeated for vice president	1856
10.	Defeated for Senate	1858

If you know your U. S. history, you will recognize this famous politician as Abraham Lincoln, who was elected the sixteenth president of the United States in 1860. Although he had many successes, which earned him a prominent place in history, he also had many failures. If he had given up after any one of these failures, he would have never won the highest elected office in the United States. His historical acclaim is due, in part, to the fact that he didn't quit!

AFFIRMATIONS FOR A POSITIVE MENTAL ATTITUDE

here may be times when the pressures in your life seem overwhelming and you find yourself losing your sense of harmony and control. At times like these, get into a comfortable position, do some deep breathing, and slowly repeat these affirmations. Read these during the day or just before going to sleep. If you choose, play soft music in the background. Repeat this exercise as often as necessary to help you reestablish your sense of feeling centered.

I am happy.

I enjoy learning.

I am an intelligent person.

I am becoming a wiser individual.

I continue to gain insight.

I am a competent and capable student.

I understand when I read and listen.

I remember what I learn.

I am achieving my goals.

I feel more confident.

I look forward to each day.

I am on the road to success.

I have time to do the things I want to do.

I relax my body, my mind, and my spirit.

My brain is filled with knowledge.

Life holds great promise!

The victory is mine!

Add your own personalized affirmations.

BECOMING AN INDEPENDENT LEARNER

he lifestyle and academic rigors of college life require great discipline as an independent learner. In college, no one gets you to your classes, sees that you are not late, makes sure that you have done your assignments, or helps you with such personal activities as doing your laundry, cleaning your room, and paying your bills.

Becoming an independent learner takes some time, but it also requires certain skills. Following are some suggestions to help you focus your energy on becoming an independent learner and experiencing academic success.

1. Learn what motivates you.
2. Know your goals.
3. Keep organized.
4. Believe that you can be successful.
5. Enhance your levels of aspiration.
6. Establish an effective study area.
7. Use many resources for learning.
8. Recognize the importance of rehearsal and review.
9. Develop higher level thinking skills.
10. Demonstrate responsibility for your education.
11. Seek opportunities for learning experiences.
12. Consider alternate possibilities.

13. Broaden your horizons.
14. Read widely.
15. Take studying seriously.

GETTING THE MOST FROM YOUR EDUCATION

 I wish I had been more serious about my education!" This is a common lament of former students who didn't make the best use of their college educational opportunities. You are encouraged to adjust your attitude, perspective, and behavior so you do not have the same regret.

Take Advantage of Opportunities

Some students arrive on campus with the attitude that a college education is a right rather than a privilege. Consequently, attending an early morning class may take second place to sleeping, or a weekend of carefree activities may cut into significant study time. Sure, you may pass your classes, but you have missed learning opportunities. Missed opportunities over several years may put you far behind those who showed up and studied for all of their classes. The detrimental effects are less easy to evaluate on a day-to-day basis, but when it comes to the job market, the competition may reveal your deficits rather quickly and openly.

Challenge Your Mind

The college experience should challenge your mind. So, take classes that are demanding and that require you to grapple with new information and compel you to think at elevated levels. Learning information is important, but building a framework for reflective, creative, and critical thinking is crucial for the future, as curiosity and exploration will continually elicit new discoveries and advanced information until the end of time. Thus, taking easy classes may get you a college degree, but it may not offer you a higher level education that will help you compete after your college years are concluded.

Earn Your Education

You earn your education by seeking and accepting responsibilities that demand use of the potential within you that has not yet been probed. College classes should be challenging because, if class content and assignments are easy, you likely have already mastered those elements. Be willing to work hard and struggle, if necessary, but resist the temptation to cheat or "buy your way through college" by hiring others to do your assignments. It may be appealing during a crisis, but, in the long run, you will appreciate the fact that you earned your education by using your own abilities. In addition, this will demonstrate leadership, initiative, and integrity as you collaborate with university personnel to design a career path of distinction and excellence. The college years will come to an end, but your reputation will follow you throughout life.

Grow Personally

The college years will provide lots of opportunities for personal growth. You likely learned much about yourself during high school; however, now that knowledge will be expanded and challenged because the college years have added new dimensions such as independence, age privileges, diversity, and new living arrangements. You will have many stresses, choices, and confrontations that will impact your values, philosophies, and security. You will encounter behaviors and lifestyles that are unfamiliar, and you will have your values challenged by learning about other cultures and customs. You will begin to understand old ideas in new perspectives, and you will find yourself in situations that take you out of your comfort zone. The opportunities for personal growth and character development are endless. Keep in mind that confidence and success, as well as frustration and failure, are important motivators and significant milestones in personal growth.

Getting the most from your undergraduate education is a one-time opportunity. Take advantage of this unique experience to monitor and evaluate your personal and academic life as you journey on the path of human development and self-actualization.

Enrichment Activities

1. Prepare a written or oral presentation to demonstrate your view on motivation.

2. Select a person you admire. Research the ways in which he or she was inspired to accomplish great things.

3. Develop a list of positive affirmations. Create affirmations for the physical, mental, emotional, and spiritual domains.

4. Share your "words of wisdom" for those who feel overwhelmed and need encouragement.

5. Using a debate format, evaluate the most effective and least effective techniques for motivation. Be sure to include broad categories such as internal vs. external, and specific elements such as verbal praise vs. a written letter of commendation.

Goal Setting

If you aim at nothing, you're sure to hit it. So the saying goes. Successful persons have a goal: they have a specific dream that they desire to turn into reality. They also are motivated to bring that dream to fruition. But, how do they do it? What does it take to set a goal and bring it into being?

IDENTIFY YOUR DESIRES

You must have a desire in order to do something better or differently than the way you are presently doing it. Many students make general statements about their desire to do better in their academic studies, but that is as far as it goes. Desires must be translated into action.

The college years may offer the first real opportunity you have had to do some serious thinking about what you want from your education. The following questions will guide you in identifying some of your academic desires and help you launch this goal-setting process.

1. What is my purpose?
2. What is my passion?
3. What inspires and motivates me?

29

4. What challenges me to achieve?

5. What are my gifts and talents?

6. What is it that I really want?

CLARIFY YOUR GOALS

nce you begin to experience a desire for academic success, it is important to clarify that desire. To help you understand what you really want and turn it into a goal, make a list of all the academic accomplishments that you would like to achieve. Begin by writing down every thought that comes into your mind. This type of brainstorming will help you sort out specific objectives.

After you make this general list, you can begin to identify the goals that are your top priorities. When you zero in on your most important objectives, prioritize them. Which ones are most important to your overall academic endeavors? Which ones can you accomplish in the short term? Which ones are long term and will take a more complex plan of action?

ESTABLISH LONG-TERM AND SHORT-TERM GOALS

f you don't know where you are going, it will be hard to plan the route. A student without a purpose is like a ship without a rudder. Each is likely to drift.

Long-range goals provide a direction and give a purpose for charting your daily course. They serve as a buffer to help you cope with short-term frustrations. Occasionally, circumstances arise that become temporary obstacles or setbacks in the pursuit of short-term academic goals. These obstacles or setbacks can become major stumbling blocks if you have no long-term goals to stabilize your focus and direct your energy.

What would you like to achieve in the next year? The next three years? The next five years? What grade point average would you like to earn? What degree would you like to obtain? These are some excellent questions to ask yourself as you embark on the task of setting long-term goals.

Short-term goals provide the beacons that light the pathways leading to our dreams. Daily objectives build character, because they require dedication, determination, and discipline. Just as great cathedrals have strong foundations, it is the daily attention to one's short-term goals that will lead to the attainment of the greater destiny. A weight lifter knows that winning top honors will require strengthening and expanding his muscles daily. Achieving academic excellence is no different; studying on a daily basis will build the necessary foundation for attaining honors in the final performance.

REMAIN FLEXIBLE

 our goals should be specific but not set in concrete. It is important to remain flexible and be prepared for the unexpected. Should the unexpected become an obstacle, be willing to make some midcourse corrections. Success is frequently not a straight road. There are often many bumps and curves with roadblocks and detours when least expected. No person can predict the unexpected. Thus, if you make your goals for success a journey as well as a destination, you will discover that your academic studies will be more rewarding.

DESIGN A PLAN OF ACTION

 fter you have clarified your specific goals, make a list of the steps that you will take to achieve each goal. These steps must be specific and should be small enough to be easily achieved on a daily basis. It is important that you "see and feel" your progress so you will be encouraged and stay motivated.

Study your past record of achievement. Compare your previous record with your new goals. Learn from your past behaviors, but be "challenged" by your new aspirations. Think big, but be realistic. It is better to revise a goal upward than to have to reduce it drastically. However, if you set your goal too low, you won't "stretch" yourself.

PUT YOUR GOALS IN WRITING

 ommit your goals and plan of action to paper. This is important since your goals will remain nebulous as long as they remain only in your head. When you make the move to put them on paper, you make a greater commitment to those goals. Putting your goals on paper gives a physical dimension to your goals to accompany the abstract ones.

Sometimes, you may want to share your goals; other times, you may want to keep them to yourself. You must decide which is best for you. Whatever your decision, write down your goals and put them where you can see them daily. Seeing your goals often will keep them in the forefront of your priorities.

Model for Goal Setting

Use the following model to assist you in putting some of your goals in writing and designing a plan of action. Once you start doing this, you will be amazed at how well this strategy works.

General Goal: To improve my grade point average.

Specific Goal: To raise my grade point average from 3.0 to 3.7 or B to A–.

Time Frame: Two semesters.

PLAN OF ACTION:
1. Increase concentrated study time by one hour per day.
2. Decrease social and "electronic" time by one hour per day. (Although the Internet, iPods, and PlayStations are great inventions, their use may consume more time than you realize.)
3. Study with others who do well or join a study group.
4. Select several classes in which to get A's.
5. Attend every class lecture and study session.
6. Decrease road trips on weekends.
7. Read and study all assigned materials in a timely manner. Take quality notes to assist comprehension.
8. Carry study cards and use on a daily basis.
9. Meet with professors two weeks before each examination. Discuss test-taking strategies.
10. Make an evaluation checklist and grade your progress on a regular basis. Make adjustments as necessary.

BE COMMITTED

 any of us fail to reach our goals because we are not really committed to reaching them. This includes being unwilling to make the sacrifices necessary to accomplish what we say we

Shoe

desire. Often, it is easier to blame others for our failures than to take a close look at what we did or neglected to do that could have been the determining factor.

For example, if you desire a better grade in a particular subject, you must be willing to spend more time in effective study. To do this, you may have to give up some of your extracurricular activities in order to devote more time to your studying. Too often we "want to have our cake and eat it too." However, if you are truly committed to a goal, you will make the ultimate effort rather than, for example, blaming your teacher for not going over the material or for making the test too hard.

EXPECT SUCCESS

here are many who don't succeed, but few who can't. A major obstacle to success is a person's expectation of failure that is more powerful than an expectation of success. In his book, *See You at the Top* (2000), Zig Ziglar says that "winning is not everything, but the effort to win is." One tends to exert more effort with an expectation of success. Thus, one very important ingredient in goal setting is to expect to succeed and then put forth the effort to bring about that success.

If you have a pattern of failure and disappointment in your academic endeavors, it may be that you are more receptive to self-defeating behaviors. If this has been the case, you will have to make a more concerted effort to change your expectations. We tend to see what we look for, and we tend to get what we expect. Therefore, look for that which is good, and expect to succeed in accomplishing the goals that you desire.

Remember, it takes as much energy to think negatively as it does to think positively. Consequently, it is better to think positively and expect success.

BE CONFIDENT

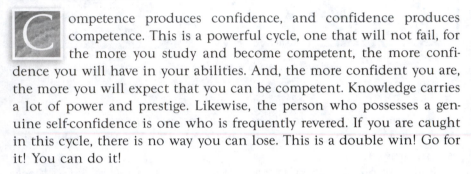

ompetence produces confidence, and confidence produces competence. This is a powerful cycle, one that will not fail, for the more you study and become competent, the more confidence you will have in your abilities. And, the more confident you are, the more you will expect that you can be competent. Knowledge carries a lot of power and prestige. Likewise, the person who possesses a genuine self-confidence is one who is frequently revered. If you are caught in this cycle, there is no way you can lose. This is a double win! Go for it! You can do it!

Enrichment Activities

1. Identify your academic goals and design a plan of action for achievement.
2. Write a short-term goal and list the components that will make up a plan for attainment.
3. Make a chart identifying several of your priority short-term goals. Keep a daily/weekly record of your progress.
4. Ponder this question: Why do I resist putting my goals in writing?
5. Demonstrate, in a creative manner, the importance of confidence in academic achievement.
6. Record three to five of your long-range goals. Put this list in a place where you can review it on a regular basis.

5

Time Management

TIME

Time is a most interesting commodity. It is an unusual commodity that can't be seen and yet can be measured. It can't be felt, and yet it can have a profound impact on individuals and the world at large. Time is a priceless resource that can't be reused; once it is gone, it is gone for good. However, time is renewable in that each day you are given a new 24 hours to use, knowing that at the end of the day those hours, too, will be gone.

Time is difficult to define and describe; in fact, the *Merriam-Webster's Dictionary* has more than 100 definitions of the word *time*. Brilliant scientists and philosophers find its definition elusive. Yet, time is something that we value, we need, and we cannot live without.

Time is an equal opportunity resource. It is perhaps the only equalizer in the human realm. No matter how important, how rich, how intelligent, or what race, color, or creed you are, you will have the same amount of time in a day as everyone else. Twenty-four hours a day and 168 hours a week are yours to use—in whatever way you choose. That's the catch! How will you choose to use your time?

Time is relative. Sometimes it goes quickly, and sometimes it seems to drag. At a party when you are having fun, time flies and the party ends all too soon. However, on Friday afternoons, time drags and classes may seem to be twice as long as they actually are. There are magic moments when we become so absorbed in what we are doing that hours seem like minutes, and then there are those moments when a minute seems like an eternity. In reality, however, each minute of each day moves at the same speed. The speed of time is out of our control. What is in our control is our management of time.

Time is a gift. Managing time is a skill. Knowing how to manage time effectively gives you a chance to spend one of your most valuable resources in any way you choose. You are in charge! Do you have time? Yes! You have 24 hours a day. But how much time you feel you have will depend on your skill in using time. It will depend on your choices, your priorities, and your ability to get the most value for each minute you spend.

A number of time management skills have proven to be effective. Take inventory of the ones that you already use and then consider adding others to your repertoire. Learning just one or two new time management skills very possibly could be keys to your more efficient use of time. In turn, you may increase your productivity and accomplish more of your goals and desires.

MONTHLY/WEEKLY/DAILY PLANNING

The Monthly Plan

Planning ahead is an important part of time management. The following steps will help you plan ahead.

1. Each month, make a graphic chart of the special activities or academic requirements you have scheduled.

2. For example, write in such activities as examinations, research papers that are due, the Homecoming Dance, and weekend travel. This will help you see the big picture.

3. Now, you will be in a better position to program your weekly schedule to include necessary time to prepare for and accommodate these specific activities.

The Weekly Schedule

Take time to plan your week. Begin by implementing the following steps.

1. Start by keeping track of a routine week of activities in relationship to time.

| Figure 5.1 | Weekly time schedule. |

WEEKLY TIME SCHEDULE

	Monday	Tuesday	Wednesday	Thursday	Friday	
8.00						8.00
8.30						8.30
9.00						9.00
9.30						9.30
10.00						10.00
10.30						10.30
11.00						11.00
11.30						11.30
12.00						12.00
12.30						12.30
1.00						1.00
1.30						1.30
2.00						2.00
2.30						2.30
3.00						3.00
3.30						3.30
4.00						4.00
4.30						4.30
5.00						5.00
5.30						5.30
6.00						6.00
6.30						6.30
7.00						7.00
7.30						7.30
8.00						8.00
8.30						8.30
9.00						9.00
9.30						9.30
10.00						10.00
10.30						10.30
11.00						11.00
11.30						11.30
12.00						12.00

2. Use the Weekly Time Schedule (see Figure 5.1) to record all of your activities. Adapt it to your individual lifestyle. Be as specific as possible. This will help you to be accountable for the small chunks of time as well as the larger chunks.

3. After you have completed a time schedule for a typical week, divide your activities into two categories. Make a list of your *Fixed* activities, such as classes, work hours, participation in religious activities, eating, sleeping, and other regular routines. Add up the number of hours and parts of hours that you use for your Fixed activities. Subtract this figure from 168 hours to calculate the approximate number of hours left in your week for study and other *Flexible* activities.

4. Next, make a list of your Flexible activities, such as recreation, socialization, television and movie viewing, and other leisure activities that you may choose to do. Divide your Flexible activities into two categories: personal time and academic time. Now add up the number of hours and parts of hours you use for Flexible personal activities and Flexible academic activities. You may be surprised to learn how much time you have for study!

Consider this example:

1. Fixed = 72
2. Flexible, Personal = 52
3. Flexible, Academic = 30
4. Total hours used: 72 + 52 + 30 = 154
5. Total hours available: 168 − 154 = 14

This means that you still have 14 Flexible hours available. How about adding a few more hours to your study schedule?

Setting Daily Priorities

Take time to plan your day. Here are some suggestions:

1. Each day make a to-do list, for example, by using the Daily Planning Guide (see Figure 5.2). List the tasks that you must accomplish.

2. Prioritize your list.

3. Arrange your list according to academic and personal priorities.

4. Organize your list into groups. For example, assume that you have to do your laundry today. Let's also assume that you have to memorize 20 words for a vocabulary test. These may be good activities to group together because you can memorize your words while you wait for your laundry to finish.

Figure 5.2 | Daily planning guide.

TO-DO LIST

1. _____
2. _____
3. _____
4. _____
5. _____
6. _____

TODAY'S PRIORITIES

1. _____
2. _____
3. _____
4. _____
5. _____
6. _____

TOMORROW'S PLANS

1. _____
2. _____
3. _____
4. _____
5. _____
6. _____

5. Cross off each item as it is completed. This will give you a feeling of accomplishment as you will readily be able to see your progress.
6. Work hard to complete your list each day. If you do not complete a task on today's list, place it as a priority on tomorrow's list.

7. Each night before you go to bed, make a tentative list of the things that you have to do the next day. This will give you a head start in organizing your upcoming day.

STUDY TIME

ime on task is related directly to academic success. Therefore, time for studying is essential to those dedicated students who seek to achieve their goals. Consider these suggestions when planning your study sessions.

1. A good general principle to follow is to spend at least 2 hours of study time for every hour you spend in class. If you spend 15 hours in class each week, plan to spend a minimum of 30 hours in effective study. Remember that school is your job; if you were employed, you would be responsible for spending time to carry out your responsibilities.

2. Organize your time in a series of short sessions. For example, it is better to spend two 2-hour sessions than spend four straight hours in study. If you should decide to spend four straight hours studying, be sure to take frequent breaks and allow time for processing the information.

3. Study in short sessions over longer periods of time. Consider this illustration: If you can study for only five hours during a week, it might be best to study an hour a day for each of the five days.

4. Set a goal for the amount of time you will spend in concentrated study time. You might consider setting a timer for 20 to 40 minutes. Then, make it a goal to focus on your study for that length of time. When the timer rings, give yourself a little break and then return for another segment of studying.

BIOLOGICAL-CLOCK STUDYING

etermine the time of the day when you get the greatest benefit from studying. Most people have a time of the day when they are most alert and a time when they are less sharp.

Pay attention to your sleep patterns, times during the day when you seem to have the most energy, and times when you seem to be a little sluggish. Then follow these suggestions:

1. Take your hardest classes during your most alert hours, if you have a choice.
2. Study during your alert hours.
3. Do routine tasks and recreational activities when your mental abilities are least effective.

Use the Weekly Subject Planner (see Figure 5.3) to record examinations and important assignments. Plan your most effective and available study times. You won't be sorry you spent the time doing this activity. The payoff will be tremendous!

TIME MANAGEMENT TIPS

he following time tips and suggestions will help you use your time more effectively.

1. Wait Time

When you have wait time, use your time effectively. Carry a card pack or notebook with you at all times so you can study your notes or memorize specific information.

2. Commute Time

Commute time can be thought of as time used to get from one place to another. We are often unaware of the time we spend in transit. Often, commuting is thought of only in relationship to automobiles or public transportation, such as riding the bus or taking the subway. However, don't forget how much time you spend walking, riding your bicycle, and using other forms of transportation.

Figure 5.3   Weekly subject planner.

WEEKLY SUBJECT PLANNER

Name _____

Week Date _____

SUBJECTS	MONDAY	TUESDAY	WEDNESDAY	THURSDAY	FRIDAY

Saturday: _____

Sunday: _____

Projects due: _____

Examinations: _____

Minutes make hours, and hours add up. So, be creative and make good use of your commute time. Here are some suggestions.

1. Commute time is an excellent opportunity to listen to tapes or CDs on topics related to your personal growth or academic studies.

2. Commute time can be used for organizing and planning your day.

3. If someone else is driving, commute time is a good time for memorizing specific information.

4. Thinking about or conceptualizing ideas for assigned projects or papers can be done while you are in transit.

5. Relaxation and contemplation are important aspects of effective learning. Remember, commute time can also be reserved for these activities.

3. Deadlines

Set a deadline for each task and do your best to stick to it. A project doesn't become an action program until you set a deadline and begin working toward it.

You might also consider setting intermediate deadlines, which could be several weeks, a week, or at least a few days ahead of the actual deadline established by your professor. This will help you get going and keep you working at a steady pace. Thus, a frantic burst of energy will not be needed at the last minute, and you may eliminate a crisis should something unexpected happen to alter your time schedule.

Remember Parkinson's Law: "Work expands to fill the time available for its contemplation."

4. Decision Making

Some decisions require lots of time for deliberation and should not be made hastily. However, many are minor day-to-day decisions and should be made as quickly as possible. If you postpone action until all objections have been overcome, you may waste a lot of time. Make your decision, move into action, and modify as necessary.

5. Interruptions

Organize your study time so you minimize interruptions. One of the benefits of concentrated activity is that you decrease the amount of time it takes to warm up for one activity and shift gears for another one. Eliminate unnecessary distractions by taking care of potential interruptions before you begin studying.

6. Meetings

If your school activities require participation in meetings, here are some important points to remember:

1. Begin and end meetings on time.
2. Stick to the agenda.
3. Try to reach some kind of decision on the designated purpose of the meeting.
4. At the end of the meeting, restate the decisions reached and any assignments given to individual members.

7. Say "No"

Be willing to say "no" to every request that does not contribute to the achievement of your goals. According to Edwin Bliss, "Of all the time saving techniques ever developed, perhaps the most effective is the frequent use of the word no" (Bliss, 1976, p. 100). Peer pressure is real and will present many demands for your time, particularly if you are talented or popular. Keep your goals in mind, and don't waste time participating in nonproductive activities.

8. Procrastination

Although procrastination will be covered in Chapter 6, no discussion of time management would be complete without bringing it to your attention. Procrastination eats time!

Usually when you procrastinate, the task mysteriously multiplies and takes far more time than it would have taken if done earlier. Even if the physical task doesn't take much time, remember that you have spent extra time thinking about the fact that you have something to do that you have not done.

> Perhaps the most valuable result of all education is the ability to make yourself do the thing you have to do when it ought to be done, whether you like it or not; it is the first lesson that ought to be learned; and however early a man's training begins, it is probably the last lesson that he learns thoroughly.
>
> —THOMAS HUXLEY

Learning to control that little force inside your head that says "This can wait until tomorrow" is absolutely necessary for academic success.

Do it now is a good phrase to memorize and use often when you are considering procrastinating. It often takes less time to do a task when you think of it or when you know you should do it than if you were to put it off. Remember, *doing it now* will save you precious minutes.

TIME-EATING TEMPTATIONS

ollege has lots of deadlines! Time is limited, however, so it is important not to waste it. Time goes quickly, particularly if you yield to "time-eating" temptations.

Use the following checklist to determine whether you are losing valuable time on these time-eating temptations. Remember that none of these activities are inherently negative. However, if they consume too much time and, thus, limit your study activities, you may need to reevaluate your academic goals and work to bring a better balance to your college life.

1. Goofing off
2. Sleeping
3. "Partying"
4. Watching television
5. Daydreaming
6. Playing video games
7. Procrastinating/worrying
8. Hanging out
9. Playing recreational sports
10. Going home on weekends
11. Talking on the telephone
12. Playing cards
13. Surfing the Internet
14. Being "in love"
15. Pursuing extracurricular activities

Add personalized statements that are not reflected on this list. Then, keep a record of time spent on these activities, and you may be surprised how much of your valuable study time is being squandered.

Frank and Ernest

Enrichment Activities

1. Debate the pros and cons of the thoughts expressed in the first section of the chapter, titled "Time."

2. Describe your most difficult aspect of time management. How will you correct this deficiency?

3. Survey the class to determine the time of day when students do their most effective studying.

4. Discuss the time-eating temptations that are your nemeses.

5. Share your best time management tips.

6. Evaluate the role that interruptions play in decreasing your study time. What can you do to minimize distruptions?

6

Procrastination

"PUT OFF UNTIL TOMORROW WHAT YOU DON'T WANT TO DO TODAY!"

This is the essence of procrastination. Procrastinators live in yesterday, avoid today, and have great plans for tomorrow. Deferrers delight in such words and phrases as "later," "soon," "next week," "when I can fit it in," "after I get this done," "when I have more time," "tomorrow," and the list goes on and on. Why the delay? What is the purpose of the postponement?

Many of the words used to identify procrastination relate to time, or more specifically, time in the future tense. However, we know that there are only 24 hours today and there will be only 24 hours tomorrow. Time is not the real factor but more likely a camouflage for something else.

There is really nothing unhealthy about procrastination itself. When you stop to think, the things you put off don't really exist. If they haven't been started, you can't postpone them. They merely remain undone.

Procrastination uses valuable energy. It takes effort to suspend the action required to accomplish a task. Moreover, most procrastinators experience some sense of guilt or anxiety. Thus, procrastination brings with it an aftermath of discomfort. This is when procrastination becomes an unhealthy and dysfunctional activity.

"I wish," "I hope," "if only," and "maybe" are convenient rationales for not doing whatever it is you keep saying you're going to do. They are escape words that continue to delude you, words that take you out of the "now" and put you into the "folly of fairyland."

You may find yourself procrastinating on occasion or as a way of life. Regardless, it is important to take a look at some possible reasons for your behavior. Procrastination is an internal enemy of accomplishment. As you gain insight into your procrastination, you will be able to conquer this college competitor.

Psychologists have varied views on the internal causes of procrastination. The key to conquering your procrastination is to understand what makes you do what you do, or perhaps what makes you *not* do what you should do! Let's take a look at some possible reasons why people procrastinate.

Fear, avoidance, self-doubt, self-delusion, blame, sympathy, and manipulation are common reasons for procrastination. Only you can determine whether one or more of these seem to fit. Be as honest as you can in your self-evaluation. You will need to come to grips with your motivations for procrastinating before you will be in a position to make some changes. It might also help to discuss these motivations with a counselor or confidant.

FEAR

 ear of the unknown, fear of success, fear of failure, fear of the difficult, and fear of the boring are all pieces of the procrastination puzzle.

1. Fear of the Unknown

If you are uncertain what a task may be like and you are not a big risk taker, you may put off the task because it is unfamiliar. Entering the world of the unknown may require change, and change is often a frightening and threatening experience.

2. Fear of Success

Believe it or not, you may be afraid of succeeding. This may sound strange because most of us struggle to succeed, but fear of success is a real phenomenon. You may be afraid of the expectations and responsibilities that will result if you do succeed. Will you be able to live up to them? Was that success a fluke, or will you be able to do it again?

3. Fear of Failure

If you begin a project, you may fail to complete it or do it well. Failure is no fun, and we all try to avoid it. But, remember the saying "nothing ventured; nothing gained." Fearing failure keeps us stuck. Ask yourself, "What is the worst thing that can happen?" So you fail. You will be able to handle it. Besides, you may succeed! Why not expect the best?

4. Fear of the Difficult

It's not easy to want to do things that may be difficult. You may have to work harder than you are used to working. Therefore, it is very easy to put off difficult projects.

5. Fear of the Boring

Sometimes you will be required to do tasks that you find boring. You don't like to do boring things, so you procrastinate!

AVOIDANCE

rocrastination allows you to avoid tasks you find unpleasant in one form or another. Avoidance is an escape mechanism. Perhaps you have run away from or have been protected from unpleasant experiences in the past and are unaccustomed to the challenges that they provide.

SELF-DOUBT

hen you put things off, you are reinforcing self-doubt. Putting something off enables you to avoid knowing whether or not you can do it. Unfortunately, lacking the confidence to tackle an unknown serves only to reinforce your self-doubt, leading to a vicious cycle. For example, saying "I'm lazy" may be a way of camouflaging self-doubt.

SELF-DELUSION

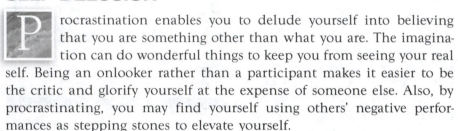 rocrastination enables you to delude yourself into believing that you are something other than what you are. The imagination can do wonderful things to keep you from seeing your real self. Being an onlooker rather than a participant makes it easier to be the critic and glorify yourself at the expense of someone else. Also, by procrastinating, you may find yourself using others' negative performances as stepping stones to elevate yourself.

BLAME

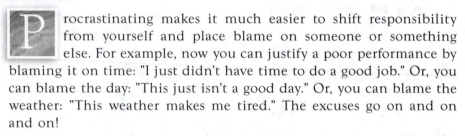 rocrastinating makes it much easier to shift responsibility from yourself and place blame on someone or something else. For example, now you can justify a poor performance by blaming it on time: "I just didn't have time to do a good job." Or, you can blame the day: "This just isn't a good day." Or, you can blame the weather: "This weather makes me tired." The excuses go on and on and on!

SYMPATHY

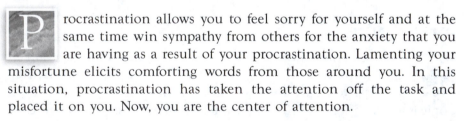 rocrastination allows you to feel sorry for yourself and at the same time win sympathy from others for the anxiety that you are having as a result of your procrastination. Lamenting your misfortune elicits comforting words from those around you. In this situation, procrastination has taken the attention off the task and placed it on you. Now, you are the center of attention.

MANIPULATION

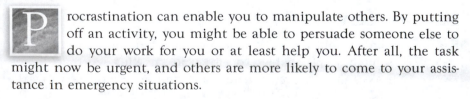 rocrastination can enable you to manipulate others. By putting off an activity, you might be able to persuade someone else to do your work for you or at least help you. After all, the task might now be urgent, and others are more likely to come to your assistance in emergency situations.

Procrastination is detrimental to those who desire achievement in academic or other endeavors. It uses energy, and it often leaves the procrastinator frustrated and the task unfinished. If you are a person who tends to procrastinate, figure out why you do, and then strive to become more proactive. If a task needs to be done, it is best to do it without delay.

Enrichment Activities

1. List and rank the internal causes of your procrastination.
2. Review the subcategories of fear. Determine which one is most detrimental to you. Evaluate the positive, negative, and neutral aspects of this choice.
3. Design a plan for overcoming detrimental procrastination.
4. Illustrate some positive aspects of procrastination.
5. Answer this question: How do I manipulate people and situations through procrastination?
6. How can you "talk yourself out of" procrastinating?

7

Deadlines

Deadlines are a necessary part of achievement! Since college is an achievement-oriented system, you will have deadlines. If you want some form of evaluation for the work that you have produced, then there must come a time when your work needs to be finished and submitted for evaluation.

You already have developed habits and strategies for coping with deadlines. These habits have developed over a long period of time. So, it would probably be wise to take a serious look at your habits—the good ones and the bad ones.

Spend a few moments thinking about the following questions, and then answer them as honestly as you can.

1. What are my feelings about deadlines?
2. How do I organize myself to meet deadlines?

These might have been some of the thoughts that came to your mind in response to the first question:

Deadlines are important.

Deadlines are made to be kept.

Deadlines can be stretched.

Deadlines can be ignored.

Deadlines are made to be broken.

Deadlines are insignificant.

Deadlines create pressure.

Deadlines cause anxiety.

Deadlines stink!

Some of the habits that you have developed are directly related to your feelings about deadlines. If you think deadlines are insignificant and can be ignored or stretched, then you may not work very hard to meet them. If, on the other hand, you think deadlines are important and should be honored, then you will keep them. Remember that your behavior is highly affected by your attitude.

In college, it will be important to honor deadlines. Some professors will listen to your reasons for procrastinating and your pleas for mercy. However, some professors will lower grades for lateness, and others simply will not accept late work. So, if you don't honor deadlines, you may put your grades in jeopardy.

Let's assume you want to honor all deadlines. How will you do it? More important, how will you do it without experiencing the anxiety of a last-minute frenzy or pulling an all-nighter?

Here is a three-step plan for coping with deadlines:

1. **Deadlines.** Record a deadline on your master calendar as soon as you know about it.
2. **Pre-deadlines.** Plan to have your project done a week, or at least a few days, ahead of the designated deadline.
3. **Stepping-stone deadlines.** Divide your project or paper into a series of stepping stones. Then, create a milestone deadline for each of these steps. Space out these milestone deadlines reasonably within the structure of your schedule.

In a sense, you are starting at the end and working backward toward the beginning. Now that you have created backward deadlines, you can work forward on your journey toward completing your goal *on time*!

Use the following illustration to help you get a better grasp of the way the three-step deadline plan works.

Problem: Writing a paper

Deadline: March 20

Pre-deadline: March 13

Shoe

Stepping-stone deadlines:

TASK	TIME GUIDE
1. Choose a topic.	Jan. 20
2. Brainstorm key ideas for topic.	Jan. 24
3. Formulate questions to guide research.	Feb. 1
4. Begin topical outline.	Feb. 5
5. Collect information.	Feb. 10
6. Make bibliography cards.	Feb. 17
7. Write a first draft.	Feb. 20
8. Seek assistance for improvements.	Mar. 3
9. Type the final document.	Mar. 7
10. Edit the final document.	Mar. 13
11. Submit the paper.	Mar. 20

By dividing larger tasks into smaller ones, you will be able to organize your time and capitalize on your creativity more effectively. Always remember to create some cushion zones in case you become ill or have some other type of emergency.

This three-step deadline plan works very well. However, like any plan, it works only if you make it work.

Enrichment Activities

1. List your feelings about deadlines. Critically discuss and evaluate the pros and cons of deadlines, and make a chart to visualize them.

2. Interview several of your professors and ask them to share their feelings about deadlines.

3. List the ways you organize yourself to meet deadlines. Share these methods with others.

4. Use the following items to evaluate your attitudes and thoughts about specific deadlines and the consequences when not met. Consider missing the deadline for a quiz, an examination, a term paper, a minor project, and a major project. Consider the consequences of having no opportunity for making up the assignment, receiving a lowered grade, making up the assignment using a different format, receiving an added assignment, making up the assignment within a given time period, or receiving a zero grade.

5. Discuss what might happen if there were no deadlines.

6. Evaluate and revise the three-step plan for coping with deadlines so that it's useful for your method of organizing yourself.

Organization

rganization is an art as well as a skill. It appears to be a natural characteristic of some people, but for others it is an overwhelming task that never gets accomplished. Good organization depends on developing good habits and is critical to achievement. It also saves time, a valuable resource. Knowing some basic principles of organization will help you in translating them into practical skills. Keep in mind that organization is an ongoing process that requires daily attention.

A place for everything and everything in its place is a good basic foundation upon which to build. Keep your system simple and functional. Also, be sure to build flexibility into your system of organization. If your system is too rigid and unforgiving, it will enslave you rather than help you.

Many different types of organization exist, each of which may require different skills. For example, your living space may require concrete organization, whereas keeping your research notes organized may need more of a mental organization. Success breeds success, so begin with one area and gradually work your way into other aspects of your life that need to be organized. Once you experience the benefits of being organized, you will be encouraged to continue the process.

I HAVE TO GET ORGANIZED!

"I have to get organized!" You likely have had this thought enter your mind more times than you can remember. Old habits die hard, and procrastination keeps you disorganized. Now is the time to *get organized!* Use these key principles to help you get started.

1. Keep a desk calendar or wall project board. Organize yourself on a daily and weekly basis so you keep a balance in your life. Keeping a weekly calendar of activities will help you see at a glance whether you are overbooking activities that are consuming time, but not moving you toward your goals.

2. Make a list of the things you need "to do." Prioritize them. Begin with the most important first. Or, do the easiest first. Or, do the hardest first. If all the things on your list need to be done, then just get them done!

3. Practice the principle of *do it now!* If it has to be done, it has to be done. So, you might just as well use the energy you would expend on thinking about it to go ahead and do it. Then, it will be done and you can get on to other things.

4. Discipline yourself to execute your decisions effectively! There are thinkers, and there are doers. Once you decide, do it!

5. Have all your materials ready before you begin a task.

6. Prepare for last-minute interruptions by not waiting until the last minute!

7. Organize your tasks into groups so you can take care of similar things at the same time.

8. Assist your memory by placing items in a specific location where you will see them as you do other tasks.

9. Think of things that have to be done and organize them in time blocks. For example, if you have a library book that is due and you have to go by the library on your way to class, take the library book with you and return it.

10. Organize and execute around priorities. Decide what is urgent and important, and do those things first.

11. Learn when to say "yes" and when to say "no."

12. Learn from good role models. Many people have excellent organizational skills that are worth emulating.

ESTABLISHING PRIORITIES

ollege life provides opportunities for experiencing many exciting activities. The new environment will offer cultural and educational ventures, athletic events, shopping, recreation, and social activities, to name but a few. All of these things are important and enjoyable parts of a balanced life.

However, balance is the key! If you study all the time, you will miss out on some very important social opportunities, but if you party too much, you will miss out on some very important study time and may jeopardize your privilege of staying in college. So, this is the time to learn the importance of establishing priorities.

This may be your first real opportunity to be on your own. You might be tempted to live it up and enjoy all of the social activities that are offered. We all like to be popular and socially accepted by our peers. Thus, the temptation is to say "yes" to every social event that is available to you so you will feel important and well liked. Unfortunately, this can be one of the biggest pitfalls for a successful academic career.

When you have not taken the time to determine your priorities, you may find that you won't have any yardstick to measure the use of your time and the wisdom of your decision making. Thus, now is the time to think about establishing your priorities.

MAKE A "TO-DO" LIST

 simple procedure to help you establish priorities is to make a list of all the things you have to do or would like to do. Many people use a "to-do" list to help them remember daily responsibilities. Our to-do list, however, is going to serve a greater purpose. So, number your paper and just start making your list. Your list might resemble the following:

1. Do laundry.
2. Return library books.
3. Make room and board payment.
4. Pay parking ticket.
5. Buy notebook.

This is an example of a typical to-do list. It is a list of the daily tasks or everyday activities that are necessary to keep your life functioning efficiently.

Shoe

However, in order to establish priorities so that you are in a better position to make wise decisions about balancing your life's activities, let's expand the to-do list concept. Continue your list. This time be sure to include some of the things you need to do and would like to do but that may be less immediate and more long term. Now, your list may include these items:

6. Read a magazine.
7. Write research paper.
8. Apply for internship.
9. Study for chemistry exam.
10. Find a part-time job.
11. Plan for spring break.
12. Go to Joe's birthday party.

You will need to prioritize all of the things "to do" that are more long term and more complex than your routine daily tasks. Look over the tasks carefully and think about their importance. Establishing priorities will be affected by the activity's purpose, the results you expect from the activity, and the activity's deadline.

Let's work with items 6 through 12 as an illustration. For example, determine that this is their order of priority:

1. Apply for internship.
2. Find a part-time job.
3. Study for chemistry exam.
4. Write research paper.

5. Plan for spring break.

6. Go to Joe's birthday party.

7. Read a magazine.

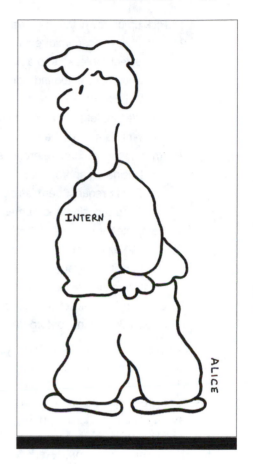

Now that your to-do list has been prioritized, list each of the five major tasks on a separate sheet of paper with the priority sequence identified. These items will now be reclassified as "projects." Since you will likely be frazzled trying to do more than four projects at any one time, you will need to get one of these partially completed before you add your fifth priority to the project list.

For each of your four priorities, you will need to make a to-do list that will relate only to that specific item. For example, applying for an internship has certain requirements, so you need to list the actions needed to accomplish this task successfully.

Now, your list might look something like this:

APPLY FOR INTERNSHIP

1. Pick up or download the forms.

2. Complete forms.

3. Get letter of academic recommendation.

4. Contact personal references.

5. Submit forms by deadline.

After you have made a list of the tasks needed to fulfill your purpose (to submit your papers on time so you will be considered for placement) and to get the desired results by the specified deadline (complete internship as scheduled so you will graduate), you will need to organize them in sequence. Here's an example.

1. Pick up or download the forms.
2. Get letter of academic recommendation.
    a. Select professors to ask.
    b. Contact selected individuals.
    c. Write letter of request.
    d. Wait for letter of recommendation.
    e. Write a note of thanks.
3. Arrange for personal references.
    a. Decide on appropriate persons.
    b. Call to request permission.
    c. Record designated names.
4. Complete forms.
    a. Make photocopies of forms if you are not completing them online.
    b. Pencil in correct information.
    c. Complete original forms.
5. Compile final packet of application documents and make copies.
6. Submit documents before deadline.

Taking the time to prioritize your tasks and organize them in such a manner will help you accomplish your goals. Having specific goals and knowing what it will take to accomplish those goals will help you make wise decisions about which activities to devote time to on any particular day or week. Tasks requiring a lot of detail, accuracy, and personal interaction often take more time than anticipated. Goals, priorities, and deadlines must be considered collectively as you seek to keep a healthy balance in your life and make wise choices about the use of your time.

Enrichment Activities

1. Create a concept map to illustrate your views on organization.
2. Describe your reasoning in determining your priorities.
3. Discuss the pros and cons of using a TO-DO LIST.
4. Design an organizational plan. Defend your plan by explaining its purpose, assumptions, information, and implications.
5. Analyze the intellectual and emotional aspects of organization.
6. What are your reasons for being organized/disorganized?

9

Brainstorming

T he word *brainstorming* literally means to storm the brain. When brainstorming, you are attempting to create a spontaneous flow of thoughts. The purpose is to produce a flood of ideas.

Companies use brainstorming techniques to come up with ideas for new products or advertising strategies. Citizen groups use brainstorming to create solutions to community problems. School systems use brainstorming to generate new ideas for curriculum and reorganization. You may have been part of a group that used brainstorming to solve a problem by spontaneously contributing ideas and then making decisions based on the best thoughts.

BRAINSTORMING AND ORGANIZATION

B rainstorming is the first and most important step in getting organized. Brainstorming takes only a small amount of thinking time but can save you a great amount of production time when you set out to do a project or an activity. Brainstorming is often overlooked and deemed unessential. However, if you are interested in saving valuable time in an already jam-packed schedule, you must not neglect brainstorming.

BRAINSTORMING FOR SUBDIVIDING

he basic purpose of brainstorming is to generate ideas through a process of free association. In relationship to organization, this can help you recognize possible solutions, identify alternative perspectives and, in addition, specify the smaller parts of the bigger task.

Often, assignments such as major projects or research papers seem like monumental tasks. This is one of the reasons students put them off longer than they should. It doesn't have to be this way. Moreover, simpler tasks that you may find difficult don't have to be neglected because you don't know where to begin. Remember, just the act of writing down your brainstorming ideas is a beginning.

Brainstorming can help you divide a larger goal into its more manageable parts so that the task will seem less overwhelming. First, define and record your goal. Next, begin to make a list of all the things you can think of that will need to be done in order to complete the goal.

GROUP BRAINSTORMING

roup brainstorming often produces a large variation in ideas due to the synergism that is created when more than one person is involved. So, if you have classmates or friends who are willing to brainstorm with you, try this activity together.

Brainstorming

Expand the following lists of synonyms for *homes* and *transportation*.

Homes

monastery	cabin
palace	attic
duplex	cave
tent	barn

Transportation

tram	submarine
kayak	helicopter
scooter	catamaran
unicycle	gondola

INDIVIDUAL BRAINSTORMING

If you are alone, however, brainstorming is still effective. Begin by making, and taking, time to think. Find a place that is conducive to thinking. Then, set aside a block of time so you don't feel rushed. Remember, it takes time for the brain to know what it is you are trying to generate. Consequently, your best solutions or ideas will often come after you think you have thought of every possible idea that could exist. Be patient! Brainstorming is as much a process as a product.

BRAINSTORMING GUIDELINES

You will need a conducive atmosphere for brainstorming. Most people do their best thinking in an atmosphere that is free from distractions. So, find a quiet, comfortable place where you

"Now, do we all have our thinking caps on?"

won't be interrupted. You will need pencil and paper, or you may wish to use a word processor.

As soon as an idea comes to your mind, write it down. Do not evaluate it. Do not judge it to be significant or insignificant. Otherwise, you will defeat the purpose of brainstorming. Just write continuously, and do not stop to edit. There are no right or wrong answers, and the order is not important. The object of brainstorming is to produce a spontaneous flow of ideas that can be used to help you effectively produce a desired product. You won't be in a position to know what ideas will be valuable until you have listed them all. So, just write them down.

Later, you will be selecting the ideas that you think are valuable and that you wish to use. For example, if you have a term paper to write or a teaching demonstration to perform, you will use the brainstorming technique to help you think of what ideas you might include and how they will fit together. If you eliminate creative thoughts early in the brainstorming process, you may throw away the very thought that could make your project unique.

PRACTICING THE TECHNIQUE

I f you have had no experience in brainstorming, spend some time practicing. Think of an object, such as a bathtub, a pencil, or a paper clip. List all of the ways that you can think of that this object could be used. In the beginning, your ideas may be quite common. However, observe how your creativity changes as you list more and more ideas.

The following items are listed to stimulate your thinking and help you see how the process works.

Problem: What are some uses for a bathtub?
1. a bathtub
2. a bed
3. a place to read
4. a place to hide
5. a flowerpot
6. a birdbath
7. a punch bowl
8. a litterbox
9. a storage chest
10. a laundry bin

Frank and Ernest

11. a little kid's pool

12. a patio garden

13. a fish bowl

14. a wagon

15. a terrarium

16. a sandbox

17. a playhouse

18. an animal cage

Now it is time for you to practice. Here's a problem for you to brainstorm, or you may prefer to think of one of your own.

Problem: What are some ways to use a paper clip? A pencil? A rubber band? A book?

UNBLOCKING BLOCKED IDEAS

 f you have trouble generating ideas, here are several unblocking techniques that writers use to help you release the floodgates so your ideas will flow easily.

1. Use a Tape Recorder

If you find that you can express your ideas orally more easily than in written form, you may want to tape-record your ideas. Dictate your ideas on a tape recorder, play them back, and transcribe them.

2. Ask a Friend, or Use a Scribe, to Write Down Your Ideas

Ask someone to write down your ideas as you speak them. Sometimes your ideas get blocked because you cannot write as fast as you can think. Someone else who writes quickly can get your ideas in print so your energies can be reserved for creative thinking.

3. Keep Writing

Keep your pencil on the paper, or your hands on the keyboard. Don't stop writing! If you can't think of any idea related to your goal, then write something else. Write your grocery list, write the days of the week, write the alphabet—write anything, but just keep writing. Often, the trouble is not beginning, but continuing. So, keep the brain in the writing mode by continuing to write.

4. Write a Letter to a Friend

If you are brainstorming in order to get started on a very important project, the pressure of beginning may cut off some of your creative juices. One of the ways you can take the pressure off yourself is to pretend that you are writing to a friend. So, rather than putting your ideas in the form of a list, put them in the form of a letter.

Here is an example of this technique.

Dear Clare,

My room is a mess! There are stacks of stuff everywhere! I have so much junk! Where do I start?

I know I need to throw some things away. I still have notebooks and old handouts from last term. If I put all my dirty laundry in the clothes bag, I could see the floor of my closet and likely find my sneakers. But, my clothes bag is such a pain. It's too tiny. Maybe if I got a big laundry basket, I could throw my clothes in it even if I were on the other side of the room. Also, I could get some more hangers, so I don't just toss my garb on the chair.

Oh, well! I think I'll go shopping. I'll clean my room later!

Hugs and kisses for Samantha and Kyle!

Love, Dr. Alice

Perhaps the informality of writing a letter to a friend will allow you to get some of your ideas on paper without feeling the pressure of performing. The format is immaterial since generating the ideas is the key purpose of this technique.

5. Evaluate Your Physical and Mental Preparation

Evaluate your external and internal preparation for brainstorming. Do you have your tools—paper, pencil, tape recorder, tapes, and batteries? Are you in an environment that is free of distractions? Have you scheduled a block of time for brainstorming? Not being prepared is often an excuse for not doing an activity. Appropriate preparation will make it easier to get the task started. Once started, it is easier to keep going.

6. Ask for Help

Sometimes it helps to have help! Don't be reluctant to ask someone to help you brainstorm. It may be that your ideas aren't flowing because you lack confidence or are evaluating your ideas before they are recorded. The ideas, support, and encouragement of a friend or family member are worth the asking.

7. Don't Quit

If at first you don't succeed, change your pace or perspective, but don't quit! You may need to take a break or do some relaxation activities to ease your tension. Just remember that brainstorming is a process. It takes time. Don't give up too easily. However, if you are not having any success after many attempts, it may be best to return to the activity another time.

Enrichment Activities

1. Choose five common objects. Organize the class into small groups and have your fellow students brainstorm uses for each object. Compare the results of the various groups.
2. Divide into pairs. Assign each pair a different object. Ask each person in the pair to come up with a list of 20 ideas for the object and then compare ideas.

3. Using the model in the chapter, write a letter to a friend in which you put some of your ideas on paper in an effort to help you get organized for a project, real or imagined.

4. Discuss the idea that "Brainstorming is as much a process as a product."

5. Write a poem or short story about "The Thinking Cap."

10

Critical Thinking

T hinking is the mind's way of creating meaning and making sense of one's internal and external world. As one starts to think, the brain begins to perform a number of cognitive processes. The realm of thinking is very complex and, thus, this discussion will be limited to just a brief overview. However, every nugget of information related to cognitive thinking is valuable and will enhance the ability of an educated person because success in college and the working world depends heavily on the ability to think. To be successful, it is important to have a large body of knowledge, but it is crucial to be able to apply that knowledge base to particular situations by using critical thinking and problem-solving techniques.

The mind gives information and response from three important areas. These are thinking, feeling, and desiring. Hence, your thoughts, feelings, and wants interact on a continual basis and have the power to influence one another in dynamic, meaningful ways. Consider this illustration. You are sitting in class and you think, "I'm bored." In order to understand this thought, you begin to evaluate your emotional state and you determine, "I'm tired." Then, you think about your desire for a nice comfortable bed and you declare, "I want this class period to end." This is a simplified example of the collaboration and integration that goes on in the mind in order to create meaning and give understanding to your particular situation.

THINKING SKILLS AND PROCESSES

here was a time when it was thought that thinking skills couldn't be taught to another person. Modern research, however, has given us a different viewpoint. Indeed, thinking skills can be learned; thus, when teachers and students make thinking a specific, direct goal of instruction and learning, good results are possible.

Thinking is a skill as well as a process. It is, however, different from the daydreaming that often is a part of study time and classroom listening. Thinking is a purposeful, conscious mental pursuit that is a natural activity for human beings. When a problem arises, the thinking process is triggered, and one begins to think of possible solutions. Thinking enables one to ask questions, evaluate answers, and create ideas that lie deep within the recesses of the mind, waiting to be explored.

Thinking takes two basic pathways. One pathway has a broad perspective and is used to generate many questions that will produce numerous ideas. The other pathway has a narrow perspective and is used to synthesize and evaluate the ideas that were generated in order to arrive at a given solution.

Thinking takes place on many levels. Much of our everyday thinking simulates daydreaming, doesn't necessitate a lot of analysis, and, therefore, is rather shallow. On the other hand, critical thinking requires that one ponder, cogitate, and deliberate. It takes more time and demands greater skill, but the results are far superior. Therefore, it seems wise to learn to think in a manner that will lead to competent, reasoned outcomes.

QUESTIONS

ritical thinking is driven by penetrating questions. Questions determine the direction and focus of thought. Questions stimulate thought if they are not limited to "yes" or "no" and dead-end answers. Thoughtful questions keep a subject or concern alive because they generate fresh ideas and foster new areas for exploration. When there are no thought-provoking questions, there is a sense of conclusion and the quest for a reasoned answer is no longer pursued.

Consider the following statement: *It is the students' responsibility to make a class interesting.* As an activity, write pertinent questions that stimulate thought-provoking ideas, generate diverse perspectives, and compel reasoned answers. Do the same for this statement: *It is the professor's responsibility to make a class interesting.* Discuss your conclusions and evaluate your questions with another classmate or

Frank and Ernest

your professor. It is important to assess your questioning abilities to determine if you need to expand your questioning skills.

TYPES OF QUESTIONS

any types of questions exist, and each one elicits a response that serves a specific purpose. As you improve your ability to ask a variety of questions, you will increase your power to cope with complex issues.

1. *Questions of fact* seek definitive, accurate information.
2. *Questions of preference* use subjective opinion based on choice.
3. *Questions of interpretation* ask one to give meaning to context.
4. *Questions of assumption* require one to state that which is taken for granted.
5. *Questions of perspective* highlight a frame of reference.
6. *Questions of implication* focus on outcomes and consequences.
7. *Questions of consistency* reveal contradictions.
8. *Questions of judgment* necessitate consideration of alternate points of view while using relevant information and sound logical reasoning.

HIGHER ORDER QUESTIONS

ritical thinkers spend more time asking higher order questions that require disciplined thinking. This type of question demands thinking that delves into the areas of assessment, analysis, synthesis, logic, and evaluation. To explore responses to these types of questions, the critical thinker will be challenged to integrate (1) knowledge of domains, (2) intellectual standards, and (3) elements of reason.

Knowledge of Domains

Complex, higher order questions often require knowledge in multiple domains. For example, perspectives from several domains may be inherent in answering a pressing question that calls for a reasoned decision. Some common domains include biology, psychology, sociology, ethics, education, medicine, law, and religion. In seeking a solution to a complex question, it would be wise to outline the various domains from which information could be sought. This practice does not mean that one person needs to be an expert in every field, but it does mean that the critical thinker needs to be aware of these domains in order to explore the many facets required of a reasoned response.

Intellectual Standards

Intellectual standards for critical thinkers require that they adhere to high-quality benchmarks. To achieve this quality of thinking, it is imperative that the thinker continually assess the criteria that form the fundamentals for good reasoned thinking. Key questions to ask include the following:

1. Is the question **clear**?
2. Is the information **accurate**?
3. Are my considerations **relevant**?
4. Are the complexities of the issue being explored in **depth**?
5. Is my thinking **logical**?
6. Is my conclusion **justifiable**?

Elements of Reason

The process of reasoning highlights the formal aspect of thinking. Reasoning takes place when the mind creates conclusions using a complex, logical framework to analyze and synthesize information and insights. Thus, when we reason, we are engaged in a conscious act of assimilation, purposefully identifying and integrating a set of elements, which forms the foundation for reasoned thinking.

Paul and Elder (2001) list eight elements essential to reasoned thought. They summarize the elements in the following two sentences: "Whenever you are reasoning, you are trying to accomplish some purpose, within a point of view, using concepts or ideas. You are focused on some issue or question, using information to come to conclusions, based on assumptions, all of which has implications" (p. 53).

As you refine your reasoning skills, you will become more proficient at recognizing the fundamental role that purpose, point of view, concepts, questions, information, assumptions, implications, and conclusions play in becoming a disciplined, critical thinker. And as you apply those skills to your learning experiences, you will become a more competent and successful student.

CASE STUDIES FOR CRITICAL THINKING

T he following case studies are provided to help you in improving your thinking about situations that occur in daily life. In each of these cases, you are asked to give your critical thinking input and advice in helping to resolve a problem or make a decision. The questions at the end of each case study will help you begin the critical thinking process. You are encouraged to think of your own questions to add to the depth of the exploration.

1. Academic Study

Peter is a freshman in high school. Although Peter considers himself to be smart, he is a student who doesn't like to study. He often takes the easy way out rather than "grapple" with the issues. He does fairly well on his daily assignments, but he doesn't study much for his tests. He is willing to "just get by" so he can get credit for high school graduation. Peter's parents are concerned and would like the school guidance counselor to initiate a plan to help Peter, who has expressed a desire to go to college, more clearly understand possible consequences of his lack of academic initiative. The school counselor has decided that a group of college students should share their thoughts and suggestions with Peter. Individuals within the group have been asked to do some critical thinking related to Peter's lackadaisical attitude and limited efforts in his academic classes.

You have been selected to be one of the students to help Peter. Respond to the following questions in preparation for your sharing session.

1. Why is this a significant issue?
2. What is your point of view?
3. What considerations are relevant?
4. What related domains need to be considered?
5. What additional information would you like to know?
6. What may be some of the complexities of this situation?
7. What advice or suggestions would you share?

2. Teacher–Student Relationships

A student and a teaching assistant discover that they are experiencing a physical attraction to one another. The student decides that these feelings are interfering with her ability to do well in her academic studies. She determines that it would be best to tell him, since they are both single adults. The teaching assistant indicates that he has the same feelings, but there is a policy forbidding any relationship while she is a student.

You have been asked to counsel the student and the teaching assistant. Respond to the following questions in preparation for your counseling sessions.

1. Why is this a significant issue?
2. What are some of the complexities of this situation?
3. What additional information would you like to know?
4. What factors should be considered now that these feelings have been shared?
5. Do you think the student should change classes? Why? Why not?
6. What might happen if the student gets a poor or failing grade?
7. Do you think this is an appropriate policy? Why? Why not?

3. Attractive Job Offer

Shawn is a Business major in his junior year of college. He is intelligent, creative, and talented. He has great knowledge in a specialized field of study that has potential for future inventions. A well-established company has offered Shawn a lucrative position with a one-year guarantee.

His future at the company would depend on the merit of his inventions. To accept this position, Shawn would need to leave college without graduating.

Should Shawn take the job offer or should he complete his undergraduate education? Respond to the following questions in preparation for helping him to make a decision.

1. What values are involved?
2. What additional information would you seek?
3. What are some significant considerations?
4. What other people should be involved in the decision? Why?
5. What might happen is he does not take the job?
6. What might happen if he does not complete his undergraduate education and obtain his degree?
7. What more would you like to know about Shawn as a person?

4. Internet Bullying

Bully is a word applied to an insolent, overbearing person who persists in taunting or tormenting another. When the Internet is used to spread defaming information in an attempt to afflict another, it is termed *Internet bullying*. Vicious information can be disseminated widely and quickly, and it is often done in an anonymous manner.

Venus is a sophomore who lives in one of the large residence halls on campus. She is very involved in campus activities and is often interviewed and quoted in the student newspaper. Some malicious rumors about Venus are starting to appear in e-mails. At first, the messages were isolated to her leadership role in student government, but now they are becoming widespread and are attacking her character.

You will need to make some decisions regarding this issue. Use the following questions to guide your thinking.

1. You receive an e-mail containing an evil rumor about Venus. What do you do?
2. Do you think Venus should read the vicious e-mails she is getting? Why? Why not?
3. What counsel would you give Venus regarding use of the Internet during this time?
4. Assume Venus is your roommate. What would you do to help her cope with this trauma?

5. Pretend you are on the Residence Hall Student Advisory Board. What would you do to deal with this problem?

6. Suppose you know the student who is doing the bullying. What legal and moral responsibilities do you have as a fellow student?

7. Assume you know who the bully is and decide to report this person to a college official. What protocol would you follow? Would you do this in person or written form?

Enrichment Activities

1. Describe your view of critical thinking.
2. Give your perspective on the following statement: "Thinking is a skill as well as a process."
3. Discuss ways in which critical thinking relates to brainstorming.
4. Evaluate your skill at asking higher order questions.
5. Think of additional questions related to intellectual standards.
6. Define a problem to be solved and list some consequences of shallow-level thinking.
7. Why do you think questioning is so important to critical thinking?

11

Listening

R eading, writing, speaking, and listening are the major categories of expressive and receptive communication skills. Formal education focuses on reading, writing, and speaking, with lesser attention paid to listening. Listening, however, is a great personal and academic resource that can be developed. Because each person has an inborn listening reflex, achieving more effective listening skills is very doable and does not require extensive study.

DEFINITION

A definition of listening states that it is to perceive by ear, usually with thoughtful and responsive attention. To hark, to heed, to hear, and to attend are other descriptive words related to the art of listening, but it is important to distinguish between hearing and listening. Hearing is a physical ability that involves recognizing the words that are being spoken; listening, on the other hand, is a skill that allows one to make sense of what someone is saying. Listening includes understanding as well as hearing. Henry David Thoreau once said, "The greatest compliment that was ever paid to me was when someone asked me what I thought, and attended to my answer" (Shafir, 2000, p. 11).

PURPOSES

Listening entails many factors and has a variety of purposes. The following lists some general purposes for listening.

1. Acquire facts
2. Learn information
3. Absorb ideas
4. Solve problems
5. Verify the accuracy of details
6. Follow directions
7. Respond with advice
8. Let others express themselves
9. Empathize with others
10. Provide a cathartic experience

BARRIERS

ome physical and psychological barriers impede listening. External factors in the environment such as temperature, noise, crowded conditions, uncomfortable furniture, emotional climate, and visual hindrances are examples. Factors such as stress, fatigue, disinterest, biases, illness, expectations, and self-doubt are examples of internal circumstances that can also interfere with one's ability to listen.

For the most part, however, it is bad listening habits that get in the way of meaningful communication and create devastating results. In preparation for a more extensive discussion on listening, evaluate yourself in relation to the following listening behaviors.
Ask yourself if you:

1. Maintain eye contact
2. Actively participate
3. Search for meaning
4. Take quality notes
5. Tolerate distractions
6. Fake attention
7. Criticize the speaker
8. Lose interest quickly
9. Take the easy route
10. Daydream

Frank and Ernest

©1998 Thaves. Reprinted with permission.

SPEAKING RATE AND LISTENING

ffective listening relies on the speaker and the listener interacting in a meaningful manner in order to accomplish the intended purpose—to communicate with understanding. It has been suggested that Americans speak at an average rate of 125 words per minute in ordinary conversations (Nichols, 1960, p. 2). When speaking before an audience, the pace slows to about 100 words per minute. People seem to be able to listen to between 400 and 500 words per minute, however. Thus, there is a large difference between speech and thought speed. Consequently, skillful and mindful listening is essential.

TIPS FOR LISTENING TO LECTURES

he average college student spends probably 12–20 hours a week listening to lectures, as this is the most common form of communicating information in the college setting. If one were to ask students if they are good listeners, the answer would likely be "yes." If those same students were asked to describe and evaluate their listening skills, however, one would likely discover that there is much room for improvement. To begin to develop the art of listening in the classroom, it is important to learn the following fundamental skills and practice their application with diligence on a daily basis.

1. Focus Your Mind

Give your full attention to the person who is speaking. It may be easy to let your mind wander for a variety of reasons. You may think that you know what is going to be said. You may be distracted by other activities around you, or your mind can get side-tracked by other thoughts, because you can think about four times faster than a speaker can talk. To keep your mind focused, think about the content rather than the delivery. Likewise, you may have to shift the position of your body, reorient your eye contact, and discipline your concentration.

2. View Listening as a Mental Task

Listening to an academic lecture is not a passive act. Genuine listening requires mental alertness that allows one to comprehend the meaning of the information that is presented. Good listeners know that meaning is gained from that which is said as well as that which isn't said. Nonverbal clues, such as body movement and facial expression, give added meaning. Listen for main ideas and supporting details, and pay attention to ideas that are repeated or emphasized. Your mind has the capacity to listen, think, take notes, and evaluate information all at the same time. For some students it may be difficult and will take disciplined practice.

3. Ask Questions to Stay Connected

During the listening process, it is crucial to ask questions. These questions may be asked internally as you strive to give meaning to the spoken word. For example, you may ask, "How does this fit with my prior knowledge of the subject?" If the professor mentions something that you do not understand, you, as a wise student, will seek clarification. A good technique is to paraphrase the speaker's idea as a lead-in to your question. Once the professor has responded, give acknowledgment and feedback using your own words as well as appropriate facial expression and body language. These are ways to demonstrate that you are actively involved in your learning.

4. Remain Objective

Excessive emotional involvement can deter one from keeping an open mind during the listening process. If one listens with bias, defensiveness, or a critical spirit, meaning will likely be skewed. Also, it should be noted that some words trigger emotionally sensitive issues. This may cause one to make an immediate judgment. Listening efficiency, therefore, drops dramatically when someone rejects an idea before completely understanding it.

Listening is crucial to comprehensive understanding and meaning-ful communication. Your academic success in college will be greatly impacted by your listening skills. Thus, any effort you make to enhance these skills will be valuable.

Enrichment Activities

1. Describe ways in which listening differs from hearing.
2. List four major barriers to listening—two internal and two external. Give suggestions for effectively coping with these hindrances.
3. Evaluate your listening habits and design a plan for improvement.
4. Discuss the interrelationship between listening and speaking.
5. Debate and defend your response to the following statement: The speaker and listener share equal responsibility for effective communication.
6. Detail the one technique that is fundamental to your listening effectiveness.

12

Notetaking Skills

M ost students take too many or too few notes. Few students know how to take good notes that will effectively serve their purpose. The quality of notetaking usually has little to do with the length or detail of the notes; instead, excellent notetaking involves the practice of discrimination. Separating the dispensable from the essential becomes a vital skill.

Although you will take notes from your textbook readings, the real test will come when you take notes during lectures. Good notes are based on good listening along with a background of knowledge that clues you into the information being presented.

KEY ASPECTS OF NOTETAKING

I t is reasonable to expect that you will spend 15 or more hours per week attending lectures. Needless to say, you will be getting a lot of auditory information. Unless you have a magnificent auditory memory, it will be necessary for you to take notes. Practice the following principles to enhance your notetaking skills.

1. Preview the Content

Before you attend class, preview the material to be presented. You might choose to read it thoroughly, particularly if you have limited prior knowledge. Or, you may choose to skim the material just before you attend the lecture. Either way, it is critical to read the material in advance of the lecture because reading ahead helps you anticipate and comprehend.

2. Know Specialized Vocabulary

It is not enough simply to hear the words spoken by the professor during class lectures. You need to comprehend the meaning of the words and the ideas they convey. Thus, work diligently to learn the specialized vocabulary of each subject so you will know what is being said.

3. Give Undivided Attention

When you are in class, put all other distractions aside and give your undivided attention to the content of the lecture. Determine that the information presented in each of your lecture classes is among the most important information you will ever receive. You will be much more successful if you make a habit of becoming absorbed in the world of each subject you study.

4. Activate Listening

Notetaking is not a substitute for listening! Before you can take good notes, you must listen well. Tune in to what you are hearing. Activating your listening will enhance your learning. Attend class to listen and learn, not just to be present.

5. Balance Listening and Writing

Knowing how to recognize the main idea and glean the key points is an extremely important skill when you are reading or listening. You need a good balance between the time you spend listening and the time you spend writing. Weigh the importance of the information. Listen for cues, such as "three major categories are," "the main idea is," or "in conclusion."

Sometimes it is good to record the words of the professor as they are used. However, it is also important that you record relevant remarks in your own words. The key is that you understand what is being said and that your notes are written in a manner that has meaning for you.

Be alert to the methods that your professor uses to present important information. For example, some information may be summarized on a PowerPoint slide or given to you as printed handouts. Listen for verbal cues and watch for nonverbal behaviors that reflect indications of emphasis or possible test questions.

6. Create Symbols and Codes

The speed with which you take notes is significant. Lecturers can talk faster than you can write. Thus, knowing shorthand or being able to generate your own style of brevity is valuable. Begin by creating specific symbols for specific classes. For example, "IR" could represent the Industrial Revolution in history class notes, and "TD" could represent thermodynamics in chemistry class notes. You might prefer to use only the beginning portion of words as a modified form of abbreviation. Another technique is to eliminate most vowels in words because the consonants form the recognition structure of a word. See if you can decipher this sentence: If u cn rd ths, u cn b a bttr stdnt. If you read the sentence—*If you can read this, you can be a better student*—you have the idea.

Drawing pictures or graphic sketches is a great way to take notes. Some students are visual learners and find that picture notes help them internalize the information. Besides, a single picture may save writing many words. Using a combination of words and pictures is best because not all content lends itself to picture notes.

7. Organize and Review Lecture Notes

Take notes in outline form or a modified form of outlining. If the lecture is not delivered in a manner that is easily outlined, then do not spend valuable time trying to determine the main points and the supporting details. Instead, just make a list of the important ideas and number them consecutively. If some points are obviously subordinate ideas, indent and list them under the main idea.

Review lecture notes as soon as possible after the class finishes. Use this opportunity to reflect on the day's lecture and fill in any pieces of information that you remember but neglected to include in your notes.

CODING SYMBOLS FOR NOTETAKING

T he following symbols are suggested for you to use as a code for one or more words. These coding symbols will help you increase the speed with which you take notes during lectures or reading periods. Many of these are standard symbols. Others are designed especially for the ease and comprehension of particular words or ideas.

You are encouraged to use these codes, or develop your own system of abbreviations. However, whatever codes you use, be sure that they are meaningful to you and they flow naturally.

+	plus
–	minus
*	important
def	definition
#	number, pounds
@	at
$	dollars, money
%	percent
=	equals, is related to
"	inches, repeated
'	feet
2	to, too, two
…	repeats same pattern
&	and
w/	with
w/o	without
ex	for example
ie	that is, therefore
re	regarding, concerning
s	summary
etc.	and so forth; in addition
4	for
be/4	before
vs	versus
wd	word
b/c	because

off the mark   by Mark Parisi
www.offthemark.com

©2002 MARK PARISI, DIST. BY UNITED FEATURE SYNDICATE, INC.

EEACX = yes   HAA = hey
NGAA = no   KAWK = stop
NAEE = maybe   ACK = OUCH
UHKA = OK
HNGHX = fine thanks
NGOO? = And you?

DENTISTRY 101

cont'd	continued
p	page
/g	to indicate "ing"

ALTERNATIVES TO INDEPENDENT NOTETAKING

ome students find it difficult to take notes while listening to lectures. Thus, much information is lost. When this situation occurs, consider alternatives. Following are some suggestions to supplement your notes.

Notetakers

1. Ask a fellow student to take notes for you. This can be done by making photocopies of the original notes.
2. Ask the professor to arrange for a student in class to volunteer to be the class notetaker. The notes are placed in a central location immediately after class so the notes can be reviewed, picked up, or copied.
3. Ask the appropriate staff person within the university to make arrangements for a notetaker. Sometimes the university will provide professional student notetakers on a paid or volunteer basis.

Taped Lectures

Caution: Get permission from the professor before taping a lecture. In some situations, you may be requested to sign a formal statement indicating that the tapes will be used only for your study purposes.

Often, it is helpful to tape lectures so you can listen to them in the privacy of a quiet, nondistracting atmosphere. However, remember that it takes time to play back lectures on a tape recording. Thus, you might consider the following suggestions:

1. Use a different tape for each class.
2. Use long-play tapes so you won't have to make changes during the lecture.
3. Label the tape with the date, topic, and name of the lecturer.
4. Use batteries so you will not be confined to a seating location that has an electrical outlet.

5. Use the pause button. Tape only the essential information.

6. Set the counter on the tape recorder at zero. Make note of the counter number when the lecturer makes a key point. Then, when you listen to the lecture, you will be alert to noting the main ideas. Also, this procedure will encourage you to keep tuned in and be an active listener.

7. Review the tape as soon as possible after the lecture. Make any necessary additions to your notes.

Enrichment Activities

1. Assign students to take notes from a class lecture. Ask them to write a summary and have a volunteer read it to the class as a review of the previous lesson. Do this on a regular basis for practice and review of important information.

2. Select a page in your textbook and draw pictures or sketches to illustrate the content. Use words sparingly.

3. Using the coding symbols for notetaking, circle the ones you use and delete the ones you rarely/never use. Present your individual favorites to your professor and classmates.

4. Make a copy of one page of your notes and give it to your professor. Ask other students to do the same. Ask your professor to post these in the classroom or share them in another format so students have the opportunity to learn from their classmates.

5. Discuss some of the issues of effective notetaking. Include the following: interest, difficulty writing and listening at the same time, speed of speaking, rate of listening, and inability to determine important information.

13

Writing Processes

A significant part of any good education involves writing, a powerful means of expressing one's knowledge and inner self in communicating with others. Reading and writing correlate highly. Reading enhances your vocabulary, and writing gives you the opportunity to use that vocabulary in meaningful ways. Thus, the more you read, the greater your vocabulary will be and the more ideas you will have to share through writing processes.

Each day of your life provides opportunities for thoughts and experiences. Your brain, in turn, becomes the storehouse and creative processor of this information. The act of writing permits the writer to explore these ideas, thoughts, and experiences on paper. The writer's task is to express them in a manner that allows the reader to comprehend and interact in meaningful ways.

The writing process and the mental processes that accompany it are tremendously complex. Therefore, in order to write successfully, it helps to understand how the writing process works and learn ways to develop the methods that will work for your individual style.

THE WRITING ACT

riting projects usually do not proceed in a steady, uniform manner. Writing is an activity that moves in a forward, backward, or sideways manner, alternating periodically throughout the project. So, be prepared to backtrack and sidestep as you proceed forward. Writing is a form of traveling, with your mind as the vehicle. Thus, anticipate detours, dead ends, and wrong turns on the writing road. Above all else, be patient, be persistent, and enjoy the journey.

WRITING PERSONALITIES

riters have different writing personalities, which are manifested in a variety of styles. Some writers will do a lot of writing in their heads before they begin to record in written form. Some writers will need to verbalize their thoughts before the thoughts become solidified and are ready for scribing. Some writers will write nonstop and complete a first draft in very few sittings. Other writers will write, then step away from the project to allow time for the ideas to incubate before returning to the writing process. Your individual style will develop as you spend more and more time writing. It is important that you find a style that works for you and then cultivate that style so it becomes natural.

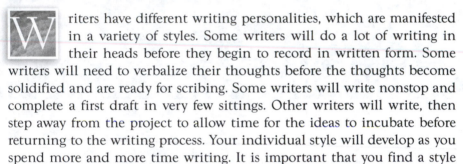

off the mark   by Mark Parisi
w w w . o f f t h e m a r k . c o m

offthemark.com

ATLANTIC FEATURE © 1995 MARK PARISI

THE DEPARTMENT OF PEOPLE WHO HAVE A CERTAIN DEGREE OF DIFFICULTY PUTTING THEIR THOUGHTS INTO BRIEF, CONCISE AND UNRAMBLING LANGUAGE

FOUR BASIC WRITING STAGES

our basic stages in the writing process include organizing, drafting, revising, and editing. The organizing stage emphasizes exploration and the planning of potential themes and supporting details. During the drafting stage, you focus on the topic you have chosen and put your thoughts in written form. The revising stage gives you a chance to revisit and refine your content and the style of writing you have chosen. The editing stage is your final opportunity to polish and perfect your project before you present it for public scrutiny.

ORGANIZING YOUR IDEAS

ransforming ideas into words and sentences that accurately portray your intentions requires good organization and a strong vocabulary. Two common strategies for organizing your information are *clustering* and *outlining*.

1. *Clustering* helps you arrange your information into main ideas and subordinate details. Also, this process helps you determine whether you have included all the main points necessary to support your thesis. The visual aspect of clustering will, in turn, assist you in arranging your ideas in a logical, sequential manner.

2. *Outlining* naturally follows the clustering process. Once you have assembled your information in appropriate groupings, you are ready to draft a tentative outline. Formal outlines follow a conventional format using Roman numerals, capital letters, Arabic numbers, and lowercase letters to show relationships and levels of importance. Many writers choose to use a modified version of outlining that uses a listing of main ideas with their supporting details.

DRAFTING, REVISING, AND EDITING

ood writers write and revise a number of times before beginning the editing phase of a project. By planning ahead, you can have the luxury of writing the first draft, letting it sit for a period of time, and then revisiting it. Returning to a project after a break from the writing process often gives a fresh perspective. Thus, each time a revision is made, the writing project likely improves.

A good thesaurus will be essential! Some students find it quicker to use an electronic device, while others still enjoy using the book format since many words can be seen at one time. A well-developed vocabulary is a powerful asset in the writing process, so take every opportunity to build your personal and academic lexicon.

During the editing stage, it is wise to have several people serve as proofreaders because you, as the writer, may be too familiar with the writing project to be objective. However, although others may assist you in the editing phase, remember that you are ultimately responsible for the content and mechanics of your paper.

MODEL FOR WRITING A PAPER

riting is a process that will require time and thought, so begin thinking about your paper as soon as you receive an assignment. Using the four basic stages of the writing process—organizing, drafting, revising, and editing—let's explore some pertinent details related to each stage.

1. Choosing a Topic

Some fundamental guidelines exist for choosing a topic for a paper. First, if you are interested in the topic, you will find the writing experience enjoyable and productive. Second, the topic must be researchable with the resources available to you. Third, it is best to limit the scope of your investigation to a particular aspect of a broader subject. Fourth, if necessary, the topic should have a perspective that can be stated in the form of a thesis or proposition.

2. Getting an Idea

A simple, straightforward way to get an idea for a writing project is to use a course-assigned or standard text for the subject area of your assignment. Turn to the table of contents or subject index, and you will find numerous entries that will give you a framework of the subject and stimulate your thought processes. Once you find a topic that sparks your interest, apply the basic guidelines for choosing a topic and you are ready to begin.

3. Preparing the Information

Once you find two or three excellent resources, use their bibliographies to give you additional books and articles to investigate. Take good notes on the information you read, but remember to keep your focus on material that is pertinent to your topic. At times, it will be reasonable to photocopy key pages that contain extensive, detailed information.

4. Incubating Your Information

Time is crucial in the incubation process. That is one of the reasons why it is important to begin writing projects early. After you have collected facts and ideas on your topic, set aside your notes for a period of time, perhaps for a week or two. During this time, your mental processes continue to work at a subconscious level. Thus, although your thinking during the incubation stage is outside your conscious attention, your brain continues to process the information.

5. Gaining Insight

Now it is time to revisit the material you gathered. You will discover that the information will be easily organized into major and minor headings that will help you form a framework for the entire paper. Likewise, you will be able to formulate an interesting introduction and the sequential arrangement as you conceptualize the complete paper.

6. Writing and Rewriting the Paper

Producing an excellent paper is the objective of this step. Your task is to turn notes and mental contemplations into the words, sentences, and paragraphs by which you will convey your thoughts and ideas to the reader in an interesting and cohesive manner. If you have trouble getting started, begin by writing from the side of your personality that is more informal and spontaneous. Soon your writing will start to flow and your paper will begin to take form. Then, you will need to revise and edit from the side of your personality that is more formal and logical.

During this step, it is normal to write and rewrite. Be willing to discard that which does not have the mark of excellence. The writing process takes patience and persistence, so keep at the task and, in time, you will create an outstanding paper.

A CHECKLIST FOR WRITING

The following checklist is provided as a guide to assist you with your writing requirements.

- ☐ 1. Use the introduction to capture the reader's attention and establish the thesis or central theme of your paper.

- ☐ 2. Organize the paper in a logical manner so the ideas flow easily from one paragraph to the next. Pay close attention to your transitions.

☐ 3. Keep the paper focused and resist letting unrelated tangents make your paper choppy and disorganized.

☐ 4. Design headings and subheadings to help the reader follow your main ideas.

☐ 5. Consider using direct quotes, properly referenced, to emphasize important points and lend authority to your thesis.

☐ 6. Rely primarily on sources and references of high quality. Your bibliography will be a showcase for your research efforts and will likely be evaluated.

☐ 7. Be sure your paper has substance by outlining the final draft and grading it as if you were the professor.

☐ 8. Check, double check, and triple check your paper for accuracy. This includes spelling, punctuation, grammar, word usage, syntax, and references.

☐ 9. Pay attention to the appearance of your paper. Visual presentation and readability will make an important first impression.

☐ 10. Rise above plagiarism and cheating and enjoy the reward that comes from being a competent writer.

The written word is a powerful form of communication. Your academic prowess is readily evident in your written expression, so take your writing seriously. Be willing to discard that which is not your very best, whether it be a paragraph, a page, or a larger portion of the project. As you enhance your skills and refine your techniques, you will enter a realm of language that will offer you endless possibilities and enjoyable rewards.

Enrichment Activities

1. Explain your writing personality in a written paper.
2. Evaluate your area of greatest weakness in the writing process. What will you do to improve it?
3. Describe some of your pet peeves about how instructors have reviewed your papers in the past. Defend some aspects of your writing that instructors evaluated.
4. Analyze the factors involved in the increased demands for excellence in writing.
5. Compare and contrast the major aspects of formal and informal writing assignments.
6. Debate the following: (1) Professors should lower a grade if there are errors in spelling and the mechanics of grammar. (2) The content is more important than the spelling and mechanics of grammar. (3) Content and mechanics are equally important in writing.

14

Study Strategies

INFORMATION EXPLOSION ERA

Like it or not, we live in an age of prodigious knowledge. The computer and the Internet have made a tremendous contribution to this vastly expanded realm. Each year, an extraordinary amount of information and technical knowledge becomes available. Textbooks are getting bigger and bigger. Some classes require that students read and study more than one text. Thus, the amount of information a student must read and comprehend within a given time frame is phenomenal!

IMPROVING READING SPEED AND COMPREHENSION

Improving your reading speed will help you cope with the vast amounts of text you will be required to read. For many reasons, some students read more slowly than is necessary to achieve complete comprehension. By recognizing that you can more often find meaning in groups of words rather than in individual words, you will understand that there is a close relationship between the rate of reading and comprehension. Thus, improvement in your rate of reading will be paralleled by the improvement in your comprehension. The outcome, however, depends on the type of material being studied, your prior knowledge, the purpose for reading, and the attention you give to the task at hand. Also, reading rapidly without focusing on useful comprehension techniques will likely be ineffective because comprehension is the cornerstone of studying. In an effort to improve your reading rate, begin by gradually increasing the speed at which you read as you monitor the desired results. Mastering these skills will be extremely valuable.

Evaluating Basic Reading Factors

You may be unaware of the factors that affect your rate of reading and comprehension. Therefore, some are listed here for your consideration.

1. If you are having trouble coping with the required reading for your classes, you may want to have your eyes evaluated by an ophthalmologist to be sure that any correctable defects are fixed before you get too far behind.

2. Develop a more efficient visual span by focusing on groups of words, phrases, and thought patterns rather than reading word by word. Remember that meaning is more often found in nouns, action verbs, and phrases, rather than in service words such as *with, is, the, of*, and *by*. Service words provide structure for the written and spoken language, but they do not carry significant meaning for comprehension. Therefore, if you choose to read those words, practice scanning them quickly.

3. Eliminate the faulty reading habit of repeatedly regressing before you finish a sentence or paragraph. It is often unnecessary to continually reread because most ideas are elaborated through a number of connections and explanations. However, if you finish a section and do not understand the concept, then reread it, as this will be purposeful rather than just habitual. If you find yourself repeatedly regressing, evaluate your power of concentration.

4. Learn to evaluate that which is important and that which is ancillary. Read the ancillary content quickly, and you will have more time to focus on significant information.

5. Realize that faulty habits of attention and retention are detrimental to reading comprehension and effective studying. When it

Frank and Ernest

comes time for examinations, you will be very happy that you have
eliminated these faulty habits. Keep in mind that memory is selective,
so read to remember and remember to read!

STRATEGIES FOR STUDYING TEXTBOOKS

any study strategies are available for you to use. Consider the
following valuable suggestions for reading and studying your
textbooks.

1. Get Acquainted with Your Book

a. Look through your book, cover to cover.

b. Read the table of contents.

c. Review the preface so you will better understand the purpose of
the text.

d. Peruse the content, chapter by chapter.

e. Evaluate the organization of the text.

f. Take note of the typographical aids, such as special headings,
graphs, charts, pictures, and italicized passages.

g. Notice the aids at the end of the book. Look at the glossary, the
appendices, the bibliography, and the index.

2. Paper-Clip Your Chapters

Place a paper clip on the first page of each chapter. This practice will
help you with your organization and will save time as you are looking
for items within a specific chapter. Also, it will give you a psychological

edge because separate chapters will seem more manageable than the whole text as one block.

3. Conduct Pre-Reading Activities

a. Define a purpose for reading.
b. Activate your prior knowledge by thinking about what you already know.
c. Look up unknown vocabulary words before you begin reading. Keep a master list of vocabulary words for each academic subject.
d. Be familiar with the author's plan of organization.
e. Organize your study area, and have all necessary study tools available.

4. Read the Chapter Summary

a. Read the chapter summary before you read the rest of the chapter. A good summary will state the important ideas in the chapter.
b. Think about what you already know in relationship to the content.
c. Think about what you would like to find out as you read the chapter. Be specific.

5. Predict Possible Test Questions

a. Anticipate test questions, and study with those questions in mind.
b. Put an asterisk in the margin next to the information that you predict will be on the test.

6. Search for Information on the Big Six

Look for information that answers the following questions: Who? What? How? Why? When? Where?

7. Use the SQ3R Method

Use the SQ3R study formula (Survey, Question, Read, Recite, Review; this is discussed in more detail later in the chapter). Apply this adaptation of SQ3R: Summary, Survey, Question, Read, Recite, Review, and Write.

a. Read the summary.
b. Survey the chapter or section.

c. Ask appropriate questions.

d. Read the chapter or section.

e. Recite the information, audibly if possible.

f. Review key portions of the text.

g. Write a summary of what you read.

8. Read a Section and Write a Summary

a. Read a section of your text and summarize the important ideas. Consider recording your summary in list form.

b. Write the information in your own words, but don't be too wordy.

c. Personalize the information so it is meaningful to you.

9. Carry on a Conversation with Your Book

a. Highlight the main ideas with a pale-colored highlighter.

b. Circle key words within the highlighted passages.

c. Number the sequences and the words that are in a list.

d. Write important points and key words in the margins.

e. Write notes of agreement and disagreement in response to the content.

f. Think of your book as a letter rather than as text. Read it expecting to react to it. Read it expecting to reread selected passages.

g. Record questions you would like to ask the author.

10. Read the Text Aloud

a. Reading is a visual process. Therefore, if you read aloud, you will be using the auditory channel as well as the visual mode of acquisition.

b. Be aware that reading aloud will likely take more time since you can see faster than you can speak.

c. Standing or pacing while reading sometimes helps concentration.

11. Draw Pictures or Designs of the Key Ideas

a. Use kinesthetic and visual methods to help you memorize the information.

b. Remember, a picture is worth a thousand words.

12. Dramatize the Information

a. Create movement and drama for the information.

b. Speak the information aloud.

c. Give information personal meaning and add emotion to make it memorable.

13. Teach the Information to Another

a. A great way to learn is to teach others.

b. Teaching the material gives you a chance to evaluate how well you know the information.

14. Focus on Structural Organizers

a. **Generalization.** Usually the main idea is presented along with the supporting details.

b. **Cause and effect.** The author gives the cause and the possible effects, or the effects followed by the cause.

c. **Comparison and contrast.** One item is compared or contrasted with another item. They may be related or unrelated.

d. **Question and answer.** The author asks a question and gives suggested answers.

e. **Sequence.** The material is listed according to some sequence, such as time, order, and significance.

f. **Enumeration.** Items of importance are placed in lists. The lists may or may not be numbered.

15. Pretend You Are the Expert

a. Enter the study situation with confidence and determination.

b. Think about or prepare a lecture plan that you would use if you were the teacher.

c. Pretend you are a famous expert and that you are reading and making notes for a world lecture.

SQ3R: STUDY STRATEGY

 Q3R is a systematic approach to studying that was introduced by Francis P. Robinson in 1941. It is an active study process that counteracts the tendency of the human mind to wander. Actually, SQ3R is a collection of study techniques compiled into a study formula that has proven very valuable (Robinson, 1941). This five-step study approach works best with expository texts that use headings and subheadings. The initials of the study strategy formula stand for:

off the mark   by Mark Parisi
w w w . o f f t h e m a r k . c o m

WELL, LA-DEE-DA! LOOK WHO GOT PROMOTED FROM A CUBICLE TO A WINDOW OFFICE...

©1999 MARK PARISI DIST. BY UFS INC. offthemark.com MarkParisi@aol.com

Survey

Question

Read

Recite

Review

SQ3R has had a number of adaptations through the years. I suggest that students expand it to be SSQ3RW. These initials stand for *Summary*, Survey, Question, Read, Recite, Review, and *Write*.

1. Summary

When beginning your study of a chapter in a textbook, read the summary first, keeping in mind the following suggestions.

a. Create a mind-set for the content.

b. Think about what you already know.

c. Relate the content to yourself—personalize it.

2. Survey

a. Look through the total chapter or passage.

b. Get a broad overview and a feeling for the content.

3. Question

a. Formulate inquiry questions using the headings to guide you.

b. Create critical-thinking questions.

4. Read

a. Read to comprehend the content and find the answers to your questions.

b. Use metacognitive monitoring to assist in comprehension.

5. Recite

a. Recite and write the key ideas.

b. Answer the questions you created at the beginning.

c. Paraphrase the passage using your own words.

6. Review

a. Check your memory by reviewing key portions of the text.

b. Understand the difference between recognizing or recalling ideas and recognizing facts.

7. Write

After reading the summary and using SQ3R, begin to *write*! Use the following key points to guide you.

a. Record key vocabulary.

b. Write meaningful ideas and comments in the margins.

c. Document main ideas, supporting details, and other significant information.

You may need to practice this strategy for several weeks before you internalize it. However, your persistence will pay off, because this strategy works!

THE INVERTED STUDY TRIANGLE

 or those of you who would benefit from "seeing" how to study your text, use the following "inverted study triangle" to help you visualize the process (see Figure 14.1).

Figure 14.1 The inverted study triangle.

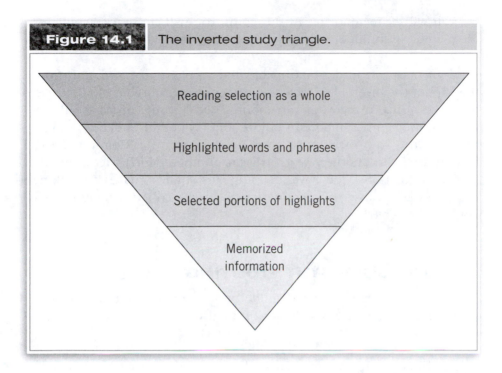

Reading selection as a whole

Highlighted words and phrases

Selected portions of highlights

Memorized information

1. The widest part, or base, of the triangle (in this case, the "base" is on top) represents all the words of the text that you will be reading.

2. The next lower section represents all the words and phrases that you will be highlighting.

3. The section below that represents the words that you will be circling or underlining with a pencil independently or within the already highlighted parts.

4. The bottom section, or "tip," of the triangle represents the portion of your work that

"If you will remember, Bobby, I urged you to study harder!"

you will be memorizing. At this point, you will create mnemonics or memory techniques to help you store key information.

To review your understanding of what you have just read, start from the "tip" of the inverted triangle and work your way back up to the base. In other words, using your mnemonics, see if you can (1) recall key words, (2) remember important points, and (3) put an understanding of the text into your own words. This process creates a "domino effect." One idea triggers another, which triggers another, which triggers another. Congratulations! You have it! Using this strategy makes test taking much easier because the information is "packaged" in a manner that lends itself to retrieval.

A STUDY GUIDE FOR STUDYING

Following are some suggested guidelines to help you monitor your studying and develop strategies for optimal learning.

- ☐ 1. I read the assigned text before it is presented in class.
- ☐ 2. I have evaluated my own study style and use that information to study effectively.
- ☐ 3. I am aware of how memory works and use metamemory strategies to monitor my own learning.
- ☐ 4. I use time management techniques to evaluate the use of my time.
- ☐ 5. I am aware of my daily biological clock and study my toughest content during my best times.
- ☐ 6. I recognize the relationship between time on task and learning.
- ☐ 7. I study for long-range retention, not just to pass the exam!
- ☐ 8. I read, study, and review on a daily basis rather than focusing on deadlines.
- ☐ 9. I use multisensory approaches for learning and retention.
- ☐ 10. I am wise in the application of memory strategies such as association, linking, mnemonics, acronyms, peg systems, story memory, picture memory, muscle memory, and fingertip memory as I study cognitive information. (See Chapter 15 for more information on these strategies.)

☐ 11. I set goals and establish the steps that will get me to those goals.

☐ 12. I personalize the information and make it meaningful to me and my situation.

☐ 13. I carry on a conversation with the author so I become an active participant rather than a passive reader.

☐ 14. I use SQ3R, SSQ3RW, or other effective study formulas.

☐ 15. I am aware of the importance of vocabulary development and have a daily and weekly plan to increase my word knowledge.

☐ 16. I recognize the role of attitude in learning and constantly evaluate my attitude as I approach each situation.

☐ 17. I am organized and plan ahead so I have plenty of time to think and process information.

☐ 18. I take notes as I read my text. I read a section and write a summary of the main ideas and supporting details.

☐ 19. I review and relate class notes to my text and text notes immediately after class is dismissed.

☐ 20. I believe that I am a capable individual and am aware that I am accountable for my own learning. I evaluate myself before I blame others. I search for solutions and take the responsibility for doing what needs to be done in order to accomplish my goals. My teachers will always recognize me as an outstanding student in body, mind, and spirit!

Enrichment Activities

1. List the five most effective study strategies that you have used to achieve good grades in high school. Evaluate these strategies in relationship to college studies. Which ones need to be changed or expanded? How will you do that?

2. What new study strategies do you intend to add to your repertoire? Why?

3. Critique each element of SQ3R. Discuss why you think this study technique has stood the "test of time."

4. How would you teach good study skills to someone who wanted to get A's?

5. Discuss the difference between "cheating" to get good grades and "studying" to get good grades.

6. Rate the role of motivation, memory, and organization in relationship to study strategies.

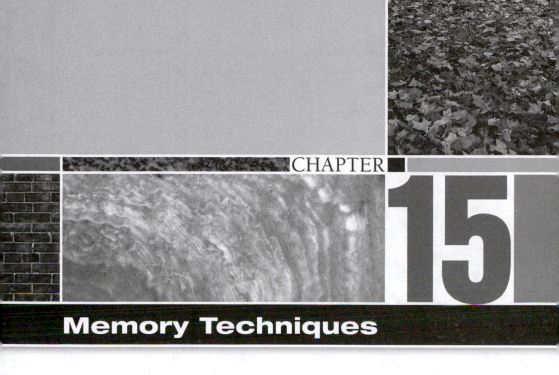

15

Memory Techniques

OUR MEMORY AT WORK

Memory is one of our most remarkable capacities! As human beings, we have the ability to think. In addition, we possess mental storage and retrieval systems that potentially are far more efficient in their capacity, flexibility, and power than the most up-to-date computers.

Sensory Input

The pace and technology of our modern life expose us to an overwhelming amount of sensory input on a daily basis. Seeing, hearing, touching, tasting, and smelling connect us to the world in which we live. Each of our senses is a complex collection of receptor cells that send out different sorts of electrical signals to the brain. Thus, our senses are the tools that enable us to discover and explore the world around us.

Processing Information

A major function of memory is to organize and process information. Different parts of the brain process different elements of an experience as we "undergo" it. This information is then classified for storage so that it can be reassembled later with all of its complex detail.

The Reality

In academic situations, you must recognize that grades are a reflection of what can be shown, not necessarily what is actually known. It may seen unfair, but if you can't recall or recognize facts or concepts in testing situations, the practical results are the same as if you had never studied in the first place. Knowing that you know is not enough. You must be able to retrieve what you know!

HOW TO REMEMBER

 good way to remember how memory works is to think of this formula: Remembering equals registration, retention, and retrieval.

1. Registration

The brain is constantly bombarded with thousands of pieces of information being collected from our sensory system. The process of registration or acquisition consists of recognizing these pieces of relevant stimuli and working to give them some type of meaning so they can be understood and stored in memory.

Registration relates closely to selective attention. You can't remember what you don't recognize or register. Acquisition also is highly dependent on exposure. The more experiences you have, the greater will be the knowledge base that you are developing. This knowledge base becomes the foundation or "glue" to which other new information is attached.

2. Retention

Rehearsal is an important component of retention. The memorizing of information consists of overt or covert repetition of information to register it more firmly into memory. Two aspects of rehearsal are *maintenance* and *elaboration*. In maintenance, you repeat the information over and over. In elaboration, you create rich associations to make the information more meaningful. It is at this stage that mnemonics clearly enhance rehearsal and likely facilitate subsequent retrieval.

3. Retrieval

Retrieval consists of two major aspects: *recognition* and *recall.* Recognition is common in multiple choice evaluations, in which the correct answer needs to be identified. Recall is needed for essay questions, in which little or no information is given.

Learning is one thing, but remembering or retrieving what you have learned can be something entirely different. Retention and retrieval strategies complement each other. Thus, the stronger the memory imprint, the greater the probability of retrieval.

STAGES OR TYPES OF MEMORY

emory is not a single system. Instead, it consists of several interconnected systems that work together. The three basic types of memory systems or stages through which information can progress are:

1. **Sensory memory.** Sensory memory is very brief—about three seconds. Its purpose is exemplified by the ability to hold the beginning letters of a word in memory while reading the ending letters so you can pronounce the entire word.

off the mark   by Mark Parisi
w w w . o f f t h e m a r k . c o m
offthemark.com

ROOKIE...

MEMORY FULL

2. **Short-term memory.** Short-term memory, although a little longer, holds information in temporary storage, just long enough to carry out a particular task such as dialing an unfamiliar telephone number. The duration of short-term memory is about 30 seconds. Its basic purpose is to give you time to decide to "use it or lose it." If you don't want to remember that particular piece of information, do nothing. If you want to use it, however, you must rehearse it in some manner to move it into the next stage, which is long-term memory.

3. **Long-term memory.** Long-term memory serves the purpose of remembering information for long periods of time. As far as we know,

its capacity is unlimited and its duration is forever! Your academic endeavors will require extensive use of long-term memory, so enhancing your memory skills will be crucial.

WRITE IT DOWN

t is a myth to think that you can remember everything that you want to remember. How many times have you thought or said, "Oh, I'll remember that!" only to forget it when you wanted to recall it. We all have been guilty of that mistake. The problem is that we repeat the same mistake over and over again!

How do we break that habit? Perhaps it is best to begin by changing the perception that only old people forget. Since you probably don't consider yourself old, you may think that of course you will remember something. And, more often than not, you will. But what if you don't? Why take the chance? Write it down!

It would be terrific if there were a lost-and-found area in the brain, much like we have in schools and other locations. If you lost an idea, you could go to the lost and found and retrieve it. However, some ideas are like fragile bubbles; if you don't do something to preserve them, they may pop and be gone forever. Write it down!

Lee Iacocca (1986) wrote in his autobiography, "The discipline of writing something down is the first step to making it happen." Think about it! If you write it down, you are more likely to get it done. Successful people everywhere make lists, write notes, or keep journals. These are all acts of writing it down.

As you practice the art of writing things down, you may discover a wonderful dividend—you will experience more ideas with less effort and anxiety. This happens for a number of reasons. First, you aren't using valuable brain energy trying to hang on to that memory. You know that you have that thought recorded, and therefore you are free to think of other things! Second, when you write it down, you can let it simmer for a period of time. Some thoughts need time to incubate. As you review your notes at another time, you may see the task or problem differently or have new ideas to add to the original thought. Third, by writing something down, you create several imprints of the item to be remembered: the initial thought, the thought written down, and a review of the thought as you actually write it.

Keep a pocket notebook handy at all times. Put one in your car, in your backpack, in your purse, on your desk, and beside your bed. You never know when you will hear or think of something that you will want to remember. Dispel the "I won't forget" attitude. Write it down!

The physical act of writing assists in memory because it is a kinesthetic/tactile and visual activity. In these days of intense academic study, you will have lots to remember, so be wise and write it down. Develop the notion that writing it down will assist your memory, help you generate more ideas, and save you time!

CHUNKING

 eorge Miller, of Harvard University, in his influential paper "The Magical Number Seven: Plus or Minus Two," pointed out that the immediate memory span is limited in the number of items it can hold (Miller, 1956, pp. 81–97).

He found that when people were given lists of either numbers or words, they had difficulty recalling more than about seven items. This is not surprising because it reflects the fact that you are unlikely to be able to subvocalize more than seven items in less than 10 seconds. Seven items is also the approximate capacity of short-term memory storage.

Miller's contribution was to point out that the number of items—not the information contained in those items—was the limiting factor. Thus, by increasing the amount of information in each item, you can remember more. In other words, you can pack a lot of information into chunks, but don't try to remember too many chunks.

Chunking is a natural process. Consider this number: 2102242. If you chunk it into two parts, you have the typical telephone number: 210-2242. Two chunks are much easier to remember than seven individual numbers. Or, consider memorizing this social security number: 123445570. It is easier to remember if you organize it into the chunks 123 44 55 70 or the chunks 123 44 5570.

Magic seven seems to be a universal phenomenon! It is a valuable tool to use when you are memorizing lists or groups of things. Remember, this concept is not limited to remembering numbers; it can also be used with words. For example, if you have to memorize a list of 20 biology words, group or organize them into chunks that have a pattern and are meaningful to you. Just remember to make each group or chunk no longer than about seven items.

MNEMONICS

Techniques for improving memory date back more than 2,000 years to the ancient Greeks, who invented a system of mnemonics. They believed that memory could be improved by mastering techniques through constant exercise and daily practice. Good memories were very important in ancient times because books, paper, and writing instruments were scarce.

The word *mnemonics* (pronounced ni-MON-iks) comes from the Greek word *mnemon*, meaning "mindful." Mnemonics are used chiefly to assist in rote memorization of lists or items in a fixed order. Mnemonics lead to a substantial improvement in memory performance for specific tasks.

Four general categories for mnemonics are words, creative sentences, rhyme and song, and special systems, such as the peg system. The following illustrations will give you an idea of how mnemonics function in memorization.

1. Words

Acronyms are words, real or created, developed by using the first letter or letters of a series of words. New information can be remembered if it is associated with something already known or remembered. Acronyms make extensive use of this associative principle. Two examples that illustrate an acronym are FACE and HOMES. FACE represents the treble clef names of the space notes in music, and HOMES represents the Great Lakes—Huron, Ontario, Michigan, Erie, and Superior.

Many words are acronyms. NASA stands for National Aeronautics and Space Administration, ZIP CODE stands for Zone Improvement Plan Code, RADAR comes from Radio Detecting and Ranging, SCUBA comes from Self-Contained Underwater Breathing Apparatus, and LASER is created from Light Amplification by Stimulated Emission of Radiation. Most people are unaware of the many words that are actually acronyms.

2. Creative Sentences

Acrostics are sentences created by constructing words that begin with the first letter or letters in a series of words. The acrostic My Very Earthy Mother Just Served Us Nine Pizzas is an excellent way to remember the planets in our solar system in order of their location from the sun. The acrostic Kids Have Dropped Dead Converting Metrics can be used to remember the length measures in the metric system.

3. Rhyme and Song

Rhyme and song have been used for centuries to teach children information. Learning the alphabet in order was often accomplished in early childhood by singing the "alphabet song." Perhaps one of the most common mnemonics to remember the number of days in each month is the classic rhyme "Thirty days hath September, April, June, and November. All the rest have thirty-one except February, which has twenty-eight." A common history fact is remembered by saying the rhyme "In fourteen hundred and ninety-two, Columbus sailed the ocean blue." Also, spelling certain words has been made easier by learning rhymes such as "I before E except after C."

Mnemonic special systems are more detailed. Therefore, peg systems using numerical association and rhyme will be explained in the next sections. Consider investigating additional writings on mnemonics as they are a valuable tool in the memory process.

THE PEG SYSTEM USING NUMERICAL ASSOCIATIONS

he *peg system* is a way to help you memorize and retain information from a list that must be learned in a specific sequence. For illustrative purposes, let's limit our example to 10 pegs, sometimes called *key words*. These 10 words will be attached to a number that acts like a peg. You will need to think about the associations until they become meaningful and then rehearse them so they will be locked into permanent memory. When you have them in permanent memory, you will be able to use them for any list of 10 items that you need to remember.

Here are 10 pegs that I have found meaningful (Olney 1988, p. 20).

1. won
2. two
3. tree
4. star

1. WON
2. TWO
3. TREE

ALICE

5. foot

6. six-pack

7. Seven-Up

8. ate

9. nine-iron

10. tent

The following are the associations that I use for the key words to make the pegs meaningful to me. (1) *Won* is a homonym of one that provides some action. (2) *Two* gives number. (3) *Tree* is three with the letter *h* left out. (4) *Star* is associated with a four-star general or a four-star hotel or restaurant. (5) *Foot* is connected to the song phrase "five foot two, eyes of blue. . ." (6) *Six-pack* is related to a six-pack of beverage. (7) *Seven-Up* reminds me of a favorite soda. (8) *Ate* is a homonym of the number eight. (9) A *nine-iron* is associated with golf. (10) Finally, *tent* is "ten" with the letter *t* added to the end to form an item that can be easily visualized.

As with any system for memory, this one has value only when it is applied with diligence. As an example, let's assume you needed to know the presidents of the United States in order. Just in case you have forgotten, the first 10 presidents are Washington, Adams, Jefferson, Madison, Monroe, Adams, Jackson, Van Buren, Harrison, and Tyler.

Now that you know the pegs and can recall them with ease, you need to spend a little time forming associations with the pegs and the names of the presidents. Remember that there are many ways to form meaningful associations, such as using alliteration, visualization, action, and ridiculous humor. Consider this example:

1. Washington won the war.

2. There were two Adams.

3. Jefferson is climbing a tree. Or, Jefferson's son is sitting in the tree.

4. Madison is one of the four stars of Madison Avenue. (You could associate Madison Square Garden and boxing since you may see stars if you get knocked out.)

5. Monroe rows his boat with his feet on Monday. (When it comes to memory, keep in mind that the brain seems to enjoy the ridiculous!)

6. Adams appears twice in the top ten so they got a six-pack to celebrate.

7. Jackson's son, Jack, likes Seven-Up.

8. Van Buren ate eight burritos in his van.

9. Harry's son was playing golf with his nine-iron.

10. Tyler was sleeping in a tent.

Once you have formed your individual associations, you may choose to link several sentences together to form a longer story. Be sure to visualize the action of the story and add a little emotion to personalize it. This will help lock the information into meaningful memory. Drawing pictures of each association may also be helpful.

Create Your Own Pegs

Make a list of your own pegs to use with the peg system.

1. _____

2. _____

3. _____

4. _____

5. _____

6. _____

7. _____

8. _____

9. _____

10. _____

THE PEG SYSTEM USING RHYME

As explained earlier, the peg system is a technique that can be used to help you memorize and retain information that must be learned in a specific sequence. This particular peg system uses the rhyme of the language as the key association for each peg or "memory hook." Other "peg sets" emphasize number relationships. It might be a good idea to memorize both sets so that you will have some options when you are confronted with memory work that involves a series of items that need to be associated.

These are the pegs that you would put into permanent memory.

1. bun

2. shoe

3. tree

4. door

5. hive

6. stick

7. heaven

8. gate

9. line

10. hen

These peg words are best learned in phrases, such as:

1. One is a bun.

2. Two is a shoe.

3. Three is a tree.

4. Four is a door.

5. Five is a hive.

6. Six is a stick.

7. Seven is heaven.

8. Eight is a gate.

9. Nine is a line.

10. Ten is a hen.

POINTS TO REMEMBER

1. A peg system is best memorized by imagining the association in a realistic or humorous manner.

2. It is best to use nouns that are meaningful to you or that follow a pattern that is easily remembered.

3. Concrete nouns are preferable to abstract ones.

4. It is best to use single nouns.

5. You may want to use a linking system to connect several pegs together in a chunk or group.

CHECKLIST OF MEMORY TECHNIQUES

ollowing is a list of techniques and key ideas that can be used to remind you of some of the many strategies developed for enhancing memory. The more strategies you know and use, the better your chances for memory success.

1. *Association.* Connect a new idea to a previous idea.

2. *Prior knowledge.* The more you know about a subject, the better your memory will function as you learn new information.

3. *Chunking.* Categorize quantities of information in groups.

4. *Numbered lists.* The brain likes numbered lists.

5. *Acronyms.* Words can be sensical or nonsensical.

6. *Acrostics.* Develop creative, expressive sentences.

7. *Picture memory.* Draw concrete pictures, and use visualization or imagery.

8. *Color coding.* Use color to organize and categorize.

9. *Personalized information.* The familiar is meaningful.

10. *Imagination.* Pretend you're the expert and very knowledgeable.

11. *Dramatization.* Drama and emotion aid memory.

12. *Kinesthetic/tactile methods.* Movement and touch assist in learning. Muscles have memory.

13. *Fingertip memory.* Touch a fingertip for each piece of information.

14. *Logic.* Organize the information in a logical manner.

15. *Ridiculous humor.* The mind enjoys a good laugh.

16. *Repeated exposures.* Review and rehearse information frequently over a period of time.

17. *Flash cards.* Carry them with you for frequent review.

18. *Repetition.* Make it varied and meaningful.

19. *SQ3R study method.* It really works!

20. *Time on task.* The more you study, the more you learn.

21. *Peg system.* Memorize a series of pegs, and attach new information to those pegs.

22. *Loci system.* Use a series of familiar locations, and associate new information with these locations.

23. *Locational memory.* Vary the places where you study.

24. *Rhyme.* Rhyme and rhythm are important elements of memory.

25. *Music.* Research supports the value of music in learning.

26. *Framed words.* Highlight, circle, or place a rectangle around a word to give it a frame and help create a focus for attention.

27. *Semantic mapping.* Draw pictures of key ideas, and illustrate their relationships.

28. *Link system.* Connect one idea to another so that remembering one item will trigger the memory of others.

29. *Story memory.* Tell a story using all the salient points that you wish to remember.

30. *Patterns.* Look for a logical pattern, a generalization, or a rule for that which needs to be memorized.

31. *Alliteration.* Memory is enhanced by words in a series that begin with the same sound.

32. *Categorization.* Memory uses a filing system to locate information.

33. *Paired association.* Couple words with a common connection.

34. *Visualization.* Create a motion picture of the significant elements of information to be learned.

35. *Self-testing.* Practice writing essays, and give yourself feedback by making up tests.

36. *Ask questions!* Search for the answers!

Remember these important precepts:

See it! Say it! Do it!
Read it! Write it! Repeat it!
Perceive it! Believe it! Achieve it!

Enrichment Activities

1. Describe your favorite mnemonics.
2. Tell what memory techniques you use most often. Why?
3. Give some illustrations related to ways you use chunking as a memory technique in your personal life and academic studies.
4. Use registration, retention, and retrieval to discuss your difficulties and successes in each category.
5. Research and write a brief paper explaining the memory process.
6. Choose one of the memory techniques from the checklist and give a verbal and visual demonstration of that technique to the class.
7. Describe why coding in visual images is important to memory.
8. Delineate the role of interest and experience in memory.

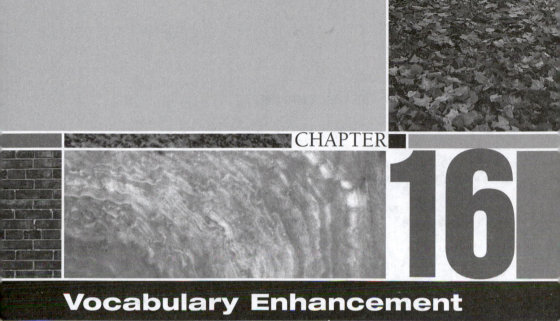

Vocabulary Enhancement

WORDS, WORDS, WORDS!

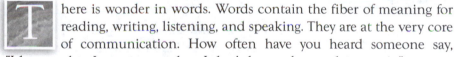

There is wonder in words. Words contain the fiber of meaning for reading, writing, listening, and speaking. They are at the very core of communication. How often have you heard someone say, "I know what I want to say, but I don't know the words to say it."

IMPORTANCE OF VOCABULARY

The importance of vocabulary development should not be underestimated. It is crucial. The poverty of some students' language is appalling considering the number of words that are accessible on a daily basis.

Think of the number of students who are prisoners of ignorance because much of the English language is foreign to them. This ignorance is not because students cannot decode, or pronounce, the words. Rather, it is because they cannot encode them.

According to James Shepherd, "There are more than 500,000 words in the English language, but it is estimated that average well-educated Americans make practical use of only about 30,000 of the words. Thus, as you pursue your college study, you must expect that any one of more

123

than 470,000 words that are unfamiliar to you may suddenly appear in the materials you read" (Shepherd, 1981, p. 47).

VOCABULARY DEVELOPMENT

ocabulary development has a horizontal and a vertical perspective. Your vocabulary bank increases horizontally as you learn new synonyms for old words. It expands vertically as you regularly add new words to your knowledge base.

1. Thesaurus

The thesaurus is a book of synonyms for words. Many thesauruses also have references to antonyms. Strictly speaking, synonyms are words that differ in form from a word but are identical in meaning to that word. However, absolute synonyms are rare. Choose synonyms carefully because, although similar in meaning or denotation, synonyms may have different connotations or interpretations. Likewise, linguistic sources and usages may differ.

2. Dictionary

A dictionary is one of the most valuable tools you will ever possess. Unfortunately, it is often used only as the last resort and is frequently devalued. A dictionary gives the pronunciation of a word, lists many different meanings, and identifies the part of speech for each specified word. Whether you use a standard dictionary, an electronic dictionary, or a computer dictionary, its value is immeasurable. Make the dictionary one of your closest companions!

RECEPTIVE AND EXPRESSIVE VOCABULARY

ou may think of yourself as having only one vocabulary, but you actually have two. You have a *receptive* vocabulary and an *expressive* vocabulary. The words that you know when you read or listen make up your receptive vocabulary. The words that you know when you speak or write comprise your expressive vocabulary.

Your receptive vocabulary is your basic vocabulary and is usually much larger than your expressive vocabulary. Even then, it is often limited. James Shepherd (1987) states that "if you have a receptive vocabulary of 14,000 words, the chances are that in 80% of what you write you rely on a vocabulary of fewer than 3,000 words and that in 95% of what you say you use a vocabulary of fewer than 1,000 words" (p. 3). Therefore, a primary goal of vocabulary development is to increase the size and understanding of your receptive vocabulary.

VOCABULARY AND COMPREHENSION

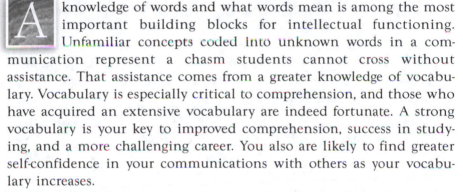 knowledge of words and what words mean is among the most important building blocks for intellectual functioning. Unfamiliar concepts coded into unknown words in a communication represent a chasm students cannot cross without assistance. That assistance comes from a greater knowledge of vocabulary. Vocabulary is especially critical to comprehension, and those who have acquired an extensive vocabulary are indeed fortunate. A strong vocabulary is your key to improved comprehension, success in studying, and a more challenging career. You also are likely to find greater self-confidence in your communications with others as your vocabulary increases.

Read the following narrative titled **A Vocabulary Story**. Be aware of the importance of vocabulary knowledge in order to achieve genuine comprehension.

A VOCABULARY STORY

Yesterday, I jumped on my **velocipede**, grabbed my **lexicon,** and **meandered** toward the park. On the way, I saw a **nefarious rapscallion** who was eating **quahogs** and **geoducks**. They smelled **pungent**.

I sat under a sycamore tree and **cogitated** my day. I really enjoyed the **tranquility** and **quiescence** of the **pristine** park. It was an **insouciant** experience.

I knew I was **procrastinating**, so I began studying my **etymology**. There was a lot of **gobbledygook** that I didn't understand, so I began to fiddle with some **palindromes** and **oxymorons.** I was feeling **bodacious**, so I created a poem, adding **alliteration** and **onomatopoeia** just to make the task a little more **complex**.

Reluctantly, I decided to head back to the dorm as I still had to do a **prodigious** amount of homework. Computing the **googols** would

Frank and Ernest

©2003 Thaves. Reprinted with permission.

take the most time and writing the report on African **pachyderms** would be the most **intriguing**.

I was **optimistic** that I wouldn't need to **sequester** myself for very long. Maybe I would have time to watch a television program before going to bed. I was glad I had avoided any **belligerent debauchery** and enjoyed a "**decadent** day!"

Sometimes you hear or read a word you don't know. When this happens, there are several things you can do to discover its meaning: (1) You can ask someone to tell you the meaning of the word; (2) you can determine what the word means by knowing the base words and its word parts; (3) you can use context clues, since often the surrounding words or ideas will provide meaning or clues to meaning; and (4) you can look for the meaning of the word in a dictionary.

THE JOY OF USING A DICTIONARY

U nfortunately, most students have not learned the joy of using a dictionary. To many, the dictionary is to be avoided. Often, the dictionary is the last resort when the meaning of a word is required, the word cannot be found in the glossary, and no one nearby knows its meaning.

1. Become Friends with the Dictionary

Becoming friends with the dictionary is one of the wisest behaviors you can develop as you strive to be successful in college. Learning to enjoy the dictionary does not have to be a long or difficult process. Actually, it can be quite simple and very rewarding. Once you learn its value, it will become one of your closest academic companions.

2. Purchase a Dictionary

Begin by purchasing a paperback dictionary that is not too elaborate. It should be medium in size but extensive enough for the college level. Be sure the print is large and as easy to read as possible. It helps if the paper will tolerate the ink of a highlighter without bleeding through the page. Keep these characteristics in mind when choosing your dictionary:

a. Paperback

b. Good-quality paper

c. Large print

d. Medium in size

Use this dictionary as your lap dictionary. Keep it close by. Make this your companion dictionary and interact with it freely and often. If you store it on a shelf, be sure you have easy access to it. You may want to carry it in your bookbag so you will have it with you throughout the day.

3. Highlight Words in Your Dictionary

When you look up a word in your dictionary, highlight the word. This technique will make the word stand out on the page. Every time you look up a word on this page or pass this page as you are looking up another word in the dictionary, you will notice the words that you have highlighted. Your eyes will automatically focus on these words, reinforcing your learning of them. By seeing them over and over, you will be setting the stage for learning, as repetition enhances memory.

4. Create a Dictionary Within a Dictionary

If the back or front of your dictionary has a page that is relatively free of print, use this page to create your own word dictionary. When you look up a word and you know that you would like to add it to your vocabulary, write it on the designated page. Record the word and a brief definition. This will provide just enough information to stimulate your memory without using too much space.

This technique is also valuable for helping you with spelling. For example, you may remember the word and its meaning, but you may be uncertain how to spell it. If you know that the word is recorded on your dictionary page, you will be able to find it more quickly. This quicker way of finding a word will encourage you to use the word more frequently and, thus, you will be more apt to incorporate it into your vocabulary.

5. Develop a Card File Dictionary

Write down words with which you are unfamiliar. Use a separate 3-by-5-inch index card for each word. Take the time to record the sentence or sentence part in which you found the word. Later on, you can look up the word and record its definition.

This is a terrific way to build your vocabulary with little effort. Your card file will also serve as an efficient way to review for your examinations, because many vocabulary words will be used in the text of the question or in the options for the answers.

Note: An excellent reference for developing word meaning is *Instant Vocabulary* by Ida Ehrlich (1988).

6. Use an Unabridged Dictionary

A large unabridged dictionary can be found in the library. This is a wonderful resource because it contains more words and provides more complete information on each word listed. It also presents a history, or etymology, of each word. This valuable information often aids in understanding the meaning of a particular word.

VOCABULARY ADVANCEMENT

Acquiring an advanced vocabulary is a lifelong process. First, it is important that you know effective ways to increase your vocabulary. Next, it is crucial that you spend time building your vocabulary. Successful students develop an interest in words. Such an interest should lead you to an enthusiasm, even a passion, for learning more about language.

How do you go about advancing your vocabulary? Although there are a number of ways, the following are a few of the most fundamental ones.

1. Vocabulary Notebook

Start a little notebook for vocabulary advancement. Let this become your developmental dictionary for receptive and expressive vocabulary.

1. Keep your vocabulary notebook handy.
2. When you see or hear a new word, write it down. You may not know how to spell it correctly, but you can always spell it phonetically—the way it sounds.
3. Look up the word in a dictionary and highlight it.
4. Talk about the word. Ask others whether they have heard the word and know its meaning.
5. Put the word on a 3-by-5-inch index card and place it in a visible location.
6. Think about the word.
7. Use the word often.

2. Vocabulary Card Pack

Start a card pack of vocabulary words. On the front side of the card,

1. Print the word in the center of the card.
2. Identify the pronunciation underneath the word using diacritical markings.

And on the back side of the card,

1. Print the word at the top of the card.
2. Record the part of speech.
3. Write the meaning of the word.
4. Use the word in a meaningful sentence to assist memory.

When you want to test yourself on your new vocabulary words, use the front side. When you want to learn the word or check your knowledge, use the back side of the card. Thus, your card pack can be used for both teaching and testing.

Carry your card pack with you throughout the day. When you have a few moments of wait time, you can expand and rehearse your vocabulary.

See how many word cards you can collect. Enjoy the fact that you are in charge of the enhancement of your vocabulary!

3. Mark New Words in Your Dictionary

Purchase a dictionary that you can mark up. When you look up a new word, mark it or highlight it with a highlighter. Every time you use your dictionary, your eyes will be drawn to the highlighted words. This type of focus will help you in rehearsing your new vocabulary, since both continual and intermittent repetition are important aspects of learning.

4. Write Key Words in Your Dictionary

Use the blank pages of your dictionary to write down new words that you look up and want to remember. This will make your dictionary more personalized and add to its value. Also, by writing down the word, you are using the kinesthetic aspect of memory. Looking at this specific portion of your dictionary will remind you of words that you are trying to remember. Also, by recording your new words, you will be encouraged by seeing a visual record of your progress.

5. Link Unfamiliar Words to Existing Knowledge

Learn how to use the contexts and meanings of word parts to make inferences about unknown words. For example, let's say you are reading a science passage and you encounter the word *carnivorous*. You do not know the meaning of the word *carnivorous*, but you know the meaning of the word *carnivore*. By using the content of the rest of the passage and the words that you already know, you will be better able to determine the meaning of the unknown word.

6. Note Multiple Meanings of Words

As many as one-third of commonly used words have multiple meanings (Devine, 1987, p. 137). Such polysemous words (that is, those with multiple meanings) create difficulties in comprehension. Make a list of polysemous words and record their various meanings. Use that list to enhance your vocabulary. Pay particular attention to figures of speech, idioms, and the like.

The following is a partial list of multiple meanings for the words **run/ran.** You may be surprised by the quantity of multiple meanings when you check a dictionary for additional illustrations.

RUN/RAN

To move swiftly (The brook runs fast.)

To move without restraint (The dogs ran loose.)

To make a quick, casual trip (I need to run to the store.)

To contend in a race (She wants to run a marathon.)

To enter an election contest (He plans to run for Congress.)

To ravel lengthwise (There is a run in her stocking.)

To play a musical passage quickly (Can you run up the scale on the piano?)

To ascend a river to spawn (The salmon are running.)

To have a persistent high temperature (I am running a fever.)

To extend in a certain direction (The boundary runs North.)

To slip through (The ship was forced to run a blockade.)

To discover by chance (I ran into a friend at the mall.)

To cause to pass (The electrician had to run a wire to an outlet.)

To print (Please run a copy of this report.)

To make oneself liable (He ran a risk when he bought that stock.)

To manage or conduct (They run their business very efficiently.)

To cause to collide (I ran into a post when I wasn't looking where I was going.)

To make a four-base hit (She hit a home run.)

To make without a miss (Everyone applauded his run in billiards.)

To accumulate before payment (I always run up a large bill at Christmas time.)

To become inefficient (We ran short of supplies while we were camping.)

To flow during a certain time (The first run of maple sap appears in the early spring.)

To thrust (He ran a sliver into his finger.)

To pursue with a purpose (The dog ran after the mailman.)

To be performed on a stage for successive weeks (The play ran for six months on Broadway.)

To become afraid (My blood ran cold.)

To draw through (He ran a thread through the eyelet.)

7. Create Semantic Maps

Make semantic maps in order to see a new word in a greater perspective. Begin by writing the key word in the center of a piece of paper. Draw a circle around the key word and attach lines extending outward. List words on the end of each line that relate to the key word. Expand each with detail.

8. Design Feature Analysis Charts

Make a chart of the characteristics of a word's meaning. Demonstrate the features of a new word by comparing and contrasting it to other members of its general class. By analyzing shared and unique features, you will add depth to your understanding.

9. Expand Whole Word Vocabulary

Pick a new word and practice using it in comfortable situations. Choose words that are interesting and fun to say. Words that have an enjoyable

Figure 16.1	Morphology of vocabulary words.
1. lexicon = a dictionary	lexi = words
2. velocipede = bicycle	veloci = speed pede = foot
3. dyslexia = dysfunction with words	dys = dysfunction lexi = words
4. polysemous = many meanings	poly = many semantic = meanings
5. quinquagenarian = of or related to the fifties	quin = five gen = kind of ian = relating to
6. triskaidekaphobia = fear of thirteen	tri = three deka = ten phobia = fear of
7. hemidemisemiquaver = a sixty-fourth note	hemi = half demi = half semi = half quaver = eighth note
8. intellectual = having knowledge	intellectu = knowledge al = relating to

rhythm and sound are frequently easier to remember. Also, choose words that are your style and that you anticipate being able to use frequently.

Here is a list of interesting words to get you started.

1. curmudgeon
2. loquacious
3. bamboozle
4. nugatory
5. pugnacious
6. equanimity
7. placate
8. facetious
9. pundit
10. syzygy

10. Build Word Power Through Structural Analysis

One of the most significant and powerful ways to build a meaningful vocabulary is to develop knowledge of the structural aspects of words. In English, as in other languages, new words are often developed by combining old words, or word parts, with affixes or existing words. Thus, once you know the meaning of a root word or word part, you can use that knowledge to figure out the meaning of other words that you don't know. Many students are not aware of this gold mine of knowledge. Not all word parts have meaning in and of themselves, but many of them do; these are the ones on which you should concentrate.

It would be wise to spend time studying the meaning-based morphemes that make up *thousands* of English words. (See Figures 16.1, 16.2, and 16.3.) Knowledge of Latin-based prefixes, roots, and suffixes, as well as Greek-combining forms, will enhance your vocabulary and make spelling much easier. With a little effort, you will be reading, spelling, and knowing the meaning of words such as these: spectroheliograph, ophthalmoscope, and pneumonoultramicroscopicsilicovolcanoconiosis!

11. Remember This Postscript

Never make the mistake of saying, "I'll never need to know that word!"
Words carry power. Your knowledge of words can empower you to move
to higher levels of achievement.

Figure 16.2	Knowledge of morphemes aids vocabulary development.
1. tele = distance/far	telephone, telegram, telepathy
2. graph = to write	lexigrapher, graphology, autograph
3. ambi = both ways	ambidextrous, ambiguous, ambient
4. helio = sun	heliology, helioscope, helioid
5. meter = measure	meter, pedometer, seismometer
6. chron = time	chronic, chronology, chronicle
7. omni = all	omnibus, omnipotent, omnivorous
8. pseudo = false	pseudonym, pseudologist, pseudodox
9. astro = star	astronomy, astronaut, astrolabe
10. cred = believe	creditable, accreditation, creed
11. ante = before	antennae, antecedent, antetype
12. vac = empty	vacuum, evacuate, vacuometer
13. pan = all	panacea, pandemic, pandemonium
14. endo = within	endocrine, endoscope, endogeny
15. migra = wander	migration, immigrant, emigrate
16. auto = self	automobile, autograph, autonomy
17. scope = to see	microscope, telescope, periscope
18. photo = light	photograph, photobiotic, photon

| Figure 16.3 | Morphemes determine word meaning. |

1. automobile	auto = self
	mobile = moveable
2. telephone	tele = distant/far
	phone = sound
3. microscope	micro = small
	scope = to see
4. biology	bio = life
	ology = the study of
5. orthodontist	ortho = straight
	dont = teeth
	ist = a person who
6. autobiography	auto = self
	bio = life
	graph = to write
7. transport	trans = across
	port = to carry
8. homograph	homo = same
	graph = to write
9. chromophobic	chromo = color
	phobic = fear of
10. geology	geo = earth
	ology = the study of
11. populicide	pop = people
	cide = to kill
12. polyglot	poly = many
	glot = tongue
13. bilingual	bi = two
	lingual = language
14. pseudonym	pseudo = false
	nym = name

Enrichment Activities

1. Discuss role models who have been influential in the advancement of your vocabulary.

2. Rate your reading and writing vocabulary. How has the strength of your vocabulary affected your academic achievements?

3. Why do you think a strong vocabulary is so essential to comprehension, speaking, and writing?

4. What specific techniques do you use to enhance your vocabulary?

5. Debate the features of the dictionary versus the thesaurus with others in your class. If you could have only one, which would you choose? Why?

6. Teach three vocabulary words to the rest of the class by using auditory, visual, and movement techniques.

7. Why are Latin and Greek prefixes and suffixes so important to vocabulary knowledge?

CHAPTER 17

Testing Guidelines

TEST ANXIETY

est anxiety may be caused by many things, including negative thinking, excessive pressure, past experiences, fear of failure, or fear of success.

Get Rid of Your Negative Thoughts

Do you find these kinds of thoughts in your self-talk?

"Tests are too hard."

"I am so stupid!"

"I can't remember anything."

"I'm afraid I'll flunk."

"I always have bad luck."

"I never do well no matter how much I study."

"My teachers and parents expect too much."

You Can Learn to Control Your Emotions

1. Think about why you become anxious or afraid.
2. Recognize that negative thoughts inhibit performance.
3. Remember that your imagination is capable of thinking about positive as well as negative images.
4. Counteract irrational thoughts with rational counterthoughts.
5. Practice deep breathing. Learn to relax.

"I looked at the first essay question and my whole life passed before my eyes."

Test Anxiety Checklist

Some test anxiety may not be a bad thing, because it may motivate you to study more. However, too much anxiety can hinder effective performance on examinations.

Use the following checklist to determine whether your anxiety is becoming excessive. Are you:

- ☐ 1. feeling overwhelmed?
- ☐ 2. having difficulty sleeping?
- ☐ 3. feeling easily fatigued?
- ☐ 4. experiencing headaches?
- ☐ 5. detecting muscle tension?
- ☐ 6. feeling out of control?
- ☐ 7. having mood swings?
- ☐ 8. blocking on information?
- ☐ 9. worrying about your ability to think?
- ☐ 10. feeling irritable or hyperactive?
- ☐ 11. having stomach or abdominal distress?
- ☐ 12. feeling unable to make decisions?
- ☐ 13. not eating, or eating too much?
- ☐ 14. experiencing feelings of despair?
- ☐ 15. being filled with frustrations?
- ☐ 16. easily moved to tears or anger?
- ☐ 17. forgetting routine information or tasks?
- ☐ 18. having difficulty concentrating?

Add personalized statements that are not reflected on the list.

If you find you are experiencing chronic anxiety, seek informal assistance, visit the counseling center, or get professional therapy.

COUNTERACTING TEST ANXIETY

 n many ways, test anxiety is a natural part of being a college student. When anxiety becomes excessive, however, it can lead to a dysfunction or to decreased academic performance.

It is up to you to take charge and do things that will decrease your anxiety and bring it into proper perspective. Following are some suggestions to help you with test anxiety.

Difficulty Sleeping

1. Keep a regular schedule as much as possible. If you find it necessary to change your schedule, try to change it at least a week before exams so you will be slightly adjusted to it before the actual week of exams. For example, if you know that you are going to have several 8:00 A.M. exams and you are not used to getting up that early, during the week before exams begin to get up at 6:30 or 7:00 A.M. so your body will have time to adjust to the change.

2. Eat the right food. Give your body proper nutrition so it can work for you and not against you. Under stress, you may be more prone to illnesses that will hinder your academic performance.

3. Cut down on caffeine and other such elements that may interfere with your sleep.

4. Exercise to reduce stress. Physical activity uses a different type of energy than does studying. Exercise uses energy that makes you physically fatigued and, therefore, helps you in falling asleep.

Waking Up Early

1. Get up and make good use of the time.

2. On the other hand, stay reclined and rest. Consider listening to music to help you relax.

Not Eating or Eating Too Much

1. Eat properly. Healthy food is essential.

2. Avoid junk food. Limit refined sugar.

3. Acknowledge any change in your eating behaviors. Recognizing the change is often enough to bring your eating back into control. If your change in eating behavior is not radical, it may not be significant. Just remember that the body functions on nutrients, so don't neglect your body. You can't perform at your best if you are not feeling well.

Headaches

1. Place a cold compress on your forehead or over your eyes. Release your lower jaw muscle. Relax your shoulders.
2. Cup your hands over your eyes. Open your eyes into the darkness of your hands. This will ease the strain.
3. Gently massage your head, neck, and shoulder area. Your tenseness may be causing a decrease in circulation.
4. Avoid the kinds of foods that could cause your headaches.
5. Soak your hands in warm water for a short time.

Hyperactivity

1. Use relaxation exercises and CDs.
2. Exercise.
3. Avoid or cut down on caffeine.

Mood Swings/Emotional Concerns

1. Recognize that exams are a time of stress and it is natural to have some shifts in your emotional state.
2. Avoid people and events that may elevate negative feelings or add to your stress. Keep your stress level as low as possible.

Depression

Consult a professional who is qualified to assist you with this difficulty.

Time

1. Determine that there is enough time to do what you need to do.
2. Plan in advance so you won't be overloaded in the days preceding your exams.
3. Use your time wisely. Study smart!

Knowledge and Thinking Concerns

1. Study effectively over a long period of time. This is the best remedy for concerns about knowing the information. If you have studied hard and well, you will most likely know the information.

2. Stay relaxed! Being relaxed will help you effectively use your thinking and reasoning powers.

3. Have confidence in your abilities. Believe in yourself.

4. Use self-talk. Repeat positive affirmations.

Blocking and Forgetting

1. Relaxation releases energy for learning and thinking.

2. Trust your memory. Practice retrieving information the same way you rehearsed storing it.

3. Practice exams on your own. Make up questions and answer them. Write out information in essay style. This type of exercise will show you what you know and what you don't know. Learn what you don't know.

4. Use visualization. Pretend that you are taking the examination. Role-play the situation in your mind. This will be like a dress rehearsal. Having experienced the examination in your mind, you may not be as anxious when you actually are taking the exam because you will already feel familiar with the task. Be sure to give yourself a good grade when you take the test in your mind. Make a physical record of the grade you would like to earn. You might want to say "Yea! Yea! I earned an A."

These suggestions should stimulate your thinking about ways you can keep test anxiety within an appropriate context. It is always important to know yourself and know your body. Be wise and logical in the behaviors that you practice. Think positive thoughts, and affirm your chances for success. Remember to consult a physician or other appropriate professional about concerns that may be beyond the normal stress of taking examinations.

TEST-TAKING STRATEGIES

or many students, taking a test is just another part of going to school or going to college. However, for some students, the worry, anxiety, or fear that taking a test elicits is overwhelming! A test-anxious student may do poorly on an exam even though he or she knows the material. Blocking or blanking out during the exam is a common response, despite the fact that the student has spent hours studying.

Preparation for the Test

1. Study for long-term retention. This is the best preparation for taking a test. Space your studying so you will have time to process information and use memory techniques effectively.

2. Find out what kind of test you will be taking, and study accordingly. Try to predict questions that might be on the exam. Look at previous tests given by the instructor and review any self-tests that may be in the textbook.

3. Make every effort to be at your best when taking the test. Adequate rest, nourishment, and physical comforts are an important part of preparation for test taking.

4. Develop confidence. Confidence comes with knowing that you are well prepared. Confidence is crucial, so spend adequate time in effective study.

General Test-Taking Tips

1. Get a good night's sleep the night before the exam.

2. Eat something nutritious the morning of the exam.

3. Dress nicely for the exam. Wear your favorite colors. A sharp appearance adds an element of confidence.

4. Arrive at the exam early, and get a good seat.

5. Avoid crash study just before the test. This may create anxiety and cause confusion. Allow your brain time to relax.

6. Look over the whole test so you can budget your time according to the value of the questions.

7. Use all of the time allotted to take the exam. Even if you just sit and stare out the window for a while, you may recall some information during this time.

Shoe

8. Trust your intuition! It usually gives good advice.

9. Use your test savvy. Give yourself credit for your knowledge and experience.

10. Be assertive, not passive, in thinking through a problem. Don't take easy defeat.

11. Think about what you know, not what you don't know. Tell yourself positive affirmations throughout the test.

12. Visualize yourself taking the test and doing well.

True–False, Matching, and Short-Answer Examinations

1. Study to memorize information and concentrate on details.

2. Look for signal or cue words, such as *all, always, never, often, basically*, and *sometimes.*

3. Take care not to add words and ideas that are not stated.

4. Remember not to ignore critical qualifiers, such as *may, should,* and *must.*

5. Eliminating incorrect or inadequate answers can narrow the field of choice.

6. Don't waste time second-guessing what the test designer might have meant. Read and relate to the words that are there.

7. When matching items, match the ones you know first; then match the ones you are unsure of or do not know.

8. Read items with double and triple negatives very carefully. Pause after each phrase and think about what it means; then, synthesize the whole statement.

9. Don't assume a piece of information is a typing error unless it is obvious. One letter can change the meaning.

10. When you recognize a statement taken directly from the book, read carefully to be sure that the instructor has not shifted the wording.

11. Statements with specific determiners such as *none* and *all* are rarely true.

12. Statements with specific determiners such as *most* or *generally* are frequently true.

13. True–false items may be determined by one word, a specific number, or a specific noun.

Multiple-Choice Examinations

1. Use two blank sheets of paper to cover the questions above and below the one you are answering. This will help you to focus.

2. Look over the whole exam quickly before beginning to answer specific questions. Determine how long the test is so that you can apportion your time appropriately.

3. Answer the easiest questions first. If you get frustrated with one section, go to a different section that may be easier for you. This encourages you and may help your brain function more clearly.

4. Don't dwell on difficult questions. Make a decision about an answer, and return later to reconsider your choice.

5. Use the process of elimination. Each time you eliminate an answer that is not correct, you increase your chances of selecting the correct answer.

6. Read the question and determine the answer before you search the multiple-choice options. Then, search for your answer. If your answer is not there, then you must choose from those that are close to your answer.

7. Search for key words that give meaning to the question or the answer. Focus on nouns, verbs, and objects, including indirect objects, direct objects, and objects of prepositions.

8. Be aware of words that specify, such as *always, never, often,* and *not.*

9. Use context, reasoning, and logic to figure out the questions you don't readily know.

10. Recognize that some questions may provide answers or clues to the answers of other questions.

11. Use your intuition to help you select an answer if you have no idea which is the correct response.

12. Collect data. If on previous tests you changed answers that were usually correct, then consider not changing an answer unless you are sure.

13. Consider answering multiple-choice questions by thinking of each choice as being true or false in relation to the question.

14. Answer multiple-choice questions with "yes" or "no" responses to each of the choices.

15. Pause throughout the test to take some deep breaths and stretch your neck and shoulder muscles.
16. Some multiple-choice questions require the best choice rather than the correct choice. Several choices may be correct, but there will be one that is most correct.

Essay Examinations

1. Use multiple-choice statements to give you ideas for answers to essay questions.
2. Be sure you know what the essay question is asking. Focus your attention on key verbs, such as *compare, contrast, describe,* and *list.*
3. Be sure to answer the question stated, not what you think is being asked. Reword the question to clarify meaning.
4. Jot down any thoughts and ideas that come to mind, and then think about how you might organize these thoughts.
5. Always explain your main ideas with supporting details. Include a clincher statement.
6. Write as much as you know! Something is better than nothing.

Remember . . . take the test! Do your best! Put your mind at rest!

Enrichment Activities

1. Which style of test do you prefer? Why?
2. Explain the interrelationship of studying, memory, and testing.
3. Share your most effective techniques for taking multiple-choice examinations.
4. Debate the use of objective test scores in determining your grade.
5. Defend the advantages and disadvantages of getting adequate rest or "pulling an all-nighter."
6. If you experience test anxiety, share the factors that impact your doing well on an examination.
7. Contemplate how a multiple-choice examination could be considered similar to a true–false examination.

18

Learning Styles

PROCESSING INFORMATION

L earning is an ongoing system of organizing, studying, and mastering the desired material. Each phase of the system has many distinct components. Think of a car, a robot, or a computer. Each has a number of unique systems that have specific functions, yet all systems must work together properly in order for the machine to function efficiently.

So it is with the human brain. The brain's two hemispheres have different but overlapping skills, or ways of processing information. You likely have a tendency to process information in a preferred manner even though both sides of the brain are working in harmony. Likewise, remember that your brain will need to integrate the information by shifting from hemisphere to hemisphere depending on the functions needed at any specific time in order to accomplish a particular task.

Following is a breakdown of some basic functions of hemispheric specialization. They are organized in pairs to assist you with the distinctions.

147

BASIC FUNCTIONS OF HEMISPHERIC SPECIALIZATION

LEFT	RIGHT
Analytical	Intuitive
Linear	Holistic
Specific	Spontaneous
Sequential	Diffused
Verbal	Nonverbal
Concrete	Symbolic
Rational	Emotional
Task-oriented	Artistic
Auditory	Visual
Logical	Creative
Thinking	Moving

Using principles of right and left hemispheric dominance, let's look at where some academic skills might be processed.

LEFT	RIGHT
Auditory/Listening	Pictures/Graphics
Phonics	Sight words
Writing	Shapes and patterns
Talking/Reciting	Touching/Moving/Doing
Order	Creativity
Language	Art/Music
Time-oriented	Not time-oriented
Focuses	Scans
Repetition/Drill	Rhythm/Movement
Details	Big picture
Blends together	Breaks apart
Two-dimensional	Three-dimensional

If you are interested in understanding more about yourself and how you process information and approach tasks, circle your preference in each pair. Determine whether most of your choices are in the right or left column. This activity will give you some indication of your hemispheric preference.

LEARNING STYLE PREFERENCE PROFILE

nstructions: Using the box on the next page and the list below, identify the statements that apply to you. Decide whether you have a strong preference for one of the styles presented. If you have a strong preference for a particular style, emphasize that style when you study. For example, if you have a preference for the visual mode, draw pictures to depict information, use charts, and watch videos to gain an understanding of the content. Also, determine whether you have a secondary preference because it may not always be possible to use your primary preference.

COMMON CHARACTERISTICS

1. Visual learners:

   . . . like visual presentations

   . . . have strong sense of color/patterns

   . . . have difficulty with auditory directions

   . . . are distracted by sound

   . . . may have artistic ability

2. Auditory learners:

   . . . prefer to listen to information

   . . . have difficulty with reading

   . . . favor verbal directions

   . . . remember words that have been spoken

   . . . like to talk

3. Kinesthetic/tactile learners:

   . . . have difficulty sitting still

   . . . prefer hands-on activities

   . . . learn better with physical activity

   . . . remember best by writing/drawing/doing

   . . . may have athletic ability

Study Characteristics Profile

Becoming an excellent student requires that you recognize your study characteristics and preferences. Although the following profile is not all-inclusive, it will give you a good overview of the characteristics related to your style of functioning. This, in turn, will alert you to how and when you need to study and what characteristics you may need to modify in order to become a more effective student.

Review the following study characteristics profile: Highlight or circle those that relate to you. Determine your basic or primary preferences and styles. Build on your strong points and work to improve areas that are weak.

1. Day Person | Mid-day Person | Night Person
2. Silence | Sound: Music   Television   Radio |
3. Auditory | Visual | Kinesthetic/Tactile
4. Short-Term Study | Long-Term Study | Cramming
5. Self-Study | Partner Study | Group Study
6. Organized | Medium Organized | Unorganized
7. Attentive | Mind Wanders | Can't Concentrate
   | | ADD   ADHD   Medication
8. Work Well Under Pressure | Buckle Under Pressure |
9. Plan Ahead | Meet Deadlines | Miss Deadlines
10. Self-Starter | Other Motivated | Unmotivated
11. Calm   Active | Overactive | Hyperactive
12. Good Memory | Weak Memory | Poor Memory
13. Good Management Skills | Weak Management Skills |
14. Sleep Needs: | 6 Hours   7 Hours   8 Hours   9 Hours   10 Hours
15. Clean Desk | Moderately Clean Desk | Cluttered Desk
16. Bright Lights | Medium Lights | Dim Lights
17. Bright Colors | Medium Colors | Dull Colors
18. Formal Seating | Informal Seating |

List other characteristics that you think are significant:

_____

_____

_____

The more you know about yourself and the way you learn, the better prepared you will be to select study and performance modes that will be most effective. Ask your professors to give illustrations in the form of your preferred style. Emphasize your strengths, and practice the styles that work best for you.

Enrichment Activities

1. Analyze your primary and secondary preferences for styles of learning. Rank the categories of Visual, Auditory, and Kinesthetic/Tactile by using the Learning Style Preference Profile.

2. Use the list of basic functions of hemispheric specialization to determine whether you have a right or left hemispheric preference.

3. List the basic teaching styles of your professors. Compare those styles to your learning style preference.

4. Determine your basic preferences by completing the Study Characteristic Profile. Individually or as a class activity, design a graph to show the study characteristics of your class.

5. How will you encourage your professors to be understanding of your learning style?

6. Synthesize and explain key features of processing information for mastery.

CHAPTER 19

Learning Difficulties

BE YOUR OWN BEST ADVOCATE!

Your high school years probably offered a greater and more structured support system than you will find in college. Therefore, you must begin immediately to develop your skills for being your own best advocate. You are responsible for your education and, when it comes to the final analysis, you will get what you negotiate.

Be "up front" about any learning difficulties. We all have disabilities in one form or another, so don't think that you are the only one in college with some type of difficulty.

Your professors will expect you to take the initiative in seeking assistance and specialized accommodations. Thus, you will need to make every attempt to understand your specific learning difficulties and discuss them with your professors.

HOW TO BE YOUR OWN BEST ADVOCATE

1. Make an Appointment Early

Make an appointment with your professor the first week or two of classes. Don't put it off! Certainly, don't wait until you run into difficulty.

This stype of timing may appear to the professor as if you are trying to weasel out of something.

Also, by consulting with your professor at the very beginning of the class, you will demonstrate your willingness to take the initiative and be responsible for your own success.

2. Document Your Learning Difficulties

If you have documentation of your learning difficulty, you may want to show the professor a copy of your diagnostic report.

It would be wise to make a list of your learning strengths and weaknesses. Be as specific as possible. Some professors have had little or no experience with college students who have learning disabilities. Thus, you may need to educate them about your specific dysfunction.

3. Anticipate Necessary Accommodations

If you know your specific needs, make a list of accommodations that you anticipate will be necessary and discuss these with your professor. (See Figures 19.1 and 19.2 for suggested forms to use.) Be reasonable, and don't ask for any accommodations that are not necessary. However, if you are not aware of the accommodations that would help you function effectively in class, it would be wise to seek counsel.

4. Remind Your Professor

If you have requested a specific accommodation that is not routine, be sure to remind the professor of your request, particularly if it might require some special arrangements. Put your request in writing.

Figure 19.1	Academic accommodations for specialized learning needs.

Student name: _____

Student number: _____

Address: _____

Telephone: _____

Curriculum: _____

    Major: _____

    Minor: _____

Academic adjustments:

    Class: _____

    Time: _____

    Professor: _____

In an effort to more accurately assess my performance in this class, I am requesting the following accommodations:

1. Extended time on examinations
2. Large-print examinations
3. Permission to write on examination booklet
4. Use of a dictionary or electronic spelling aid, if spelling is evaluated
5. A quiet area or headphones to block out extraneous noises during examinations
6. Use of an area with limited visual distractions during examinations
7. Use of a reader
8. Use of a tape recorder/notetaker
9. Clarification of directions/assignments
10. Extended time on project/paper/assignment

Other accommodations being requested:

_____

_____

If you would like a reference, please feel free to contact:

Name: _____

Address: _____

Telephone: _____

Signature: _____

| Figure 19.2 | Learning accommodations interaction form. |

To: (Professor) _____

From: (Student) _____

Dear Professor:

I am enrolled in the class _____ , which meets on

_____ at _____.

A. My learning strengths are:

    1. _____

    2. _____

    3. _____

    4. _____

    5. _____

B. In academic settings, I experience the following difficulties:

    1. _____

    2. _____

    3. _____

    4. _____

    5. _____

C. To enhance my chances for success in this class, I would benefit from the following accommodations:

    1. _____

    _____

    2. _____

    _____

    3. _____

    _____

If you need further information, please contact me at:

_____

Sincerely,

_____

Date: _____

5. Use the Resources of the University

The university community has many available resources. If you need assistance, be sure to ask. (See Figure 19.3.)

COLLEGE ACCOMMODATIONS FOR STUDENTS WITH LEARNING DIFFICULTIES

Students with learning difficulties, either diagnosed or undiagnosed, are entering colleges at an ever-increasing rate. Many will identify themselves. Others will be concerned that they will be unfairly judged if they identify the fact that they have a learning disorder. Still others will enter college without specifically knowing they have a learning disability and will not be diagnosed until after they begin their college studies.

Regardless of the circumstances, colleges must address the needs of the students within the college community. The Office of Civil Rights of the Department of Education requires that every college receiving federal funds of any kind have a Section 504 Coordinator. Section 504 of the Rehabilitation Act of 1973 states that "no otherwise qualified handicapped individual . . . shall, solely by reason of his handicap, be excluded from the participation in, be denied the benefits of, or be subjected to discrimination under any program or activity receiving federal financial assistance" (Scheiber and Talpers, 1987, p. viii). Thus, colleges and universities are required to make "reasonable adjustments" to ensure that students with learning difficulties are not excluded from programs because of the absence of ancillary aids.

No two students with learning difficulties are alike and, thus, not all will need the same accommodations. However, some common accommodations, if provided, are of great value to the student with learning difficulties and are invaluable in contributing to a successful completion of a college education.

Page 159 offers a list of common accommodations that have proven invaluable to students with learning difficulties, including dyslexia. Some are more significant than others because they have a direct impact on the requirements of the college curriculum or the criteria necessary to complete a college degree. Students without learning difficulties may profit little from these accommodations. For the student with learning difficulties, however, these accommodations may mean the difference between success and failure or between acceptable and unacceptable work.

Figure 19.3	University resources.

1. Academic/Special Services Center:

   Contact Person: _____

   Building: _____ Telephone: _____

2. Counseling Center:

   Counselor: _____

   Building: _____ Telephone: _____

3. Academic Advisor:

   Professor: _____

   Building: _____ Telephone: _____

4. Major Advisor:

   Professor: _____

   Building: _____ Telephone: _____

5. Minor Advisor:

   Professor: _____

   Building: _____ Telephone: _____

6. Office of Student Life:

   Director: _____

   Building: _____ Telephone: _____

7. Department Office:

   Chairperson: _____

   Building: _____ Telephone: _____

8. Individual Mentors:

   Name: _____ Telephone: _____

   Name: _____ Telephone: _____

1. **Extended time on examinations.** By far the most commonly requested accommodation is extended time on examinations. This request is essential due to the slower reading rate and information-processing difficulties of many students with learning disorders. Moreover, if the examination involves writing, more time will be required to conceptualize and organize the written content.

2. **Quiet location.** Some students have been diagnosed with an attention deficit disorder. This means they will likely have difficulty concentrating because they are easily distracted by background sounds or the motion of those around them. Taking examinations in a quiet location, free from distractions, will be imperative if students are to have a reasonable chance of doing their best.

3. **Alternate forms of examinations.** Since examinations are a primary means of evaluating success in a college course, the student and professor should discuss examination accommodations so that the results will be a more accurate reflection of the knowledge and achievement of the student. Multiple-choice examinations may be particularly difficult for some students while, for others, writing essay answers presents a real quandary. Some adjustments that may be valuable include allowing the student to ask for clarification of the written directions or test questions, having the test tape-recorded so it can be processed auditorily as well as visually, furnishing a reader for the examination, and allowing the student to be tested by an alternative form of testing.

4. **Use of a laptop computer.** The physical act of writing while conceptualizing thoughts at the same time is difficult for some students. Consequently, the students' writing may be hard to decipher, and their thoughts less organized. Students sometimes find it easier to mechanically construct thoughts rather than form them with script. While assistive technologies are not a panacea, they do provide valuable tools that can help students express more of their potential. Thus, if physical writing presents a significant problem, it would be valuable to allow the student to use a word processor of some type.

5. **Use of an electronic spelling aid or dictionary.** It is well documented that spelling correctly is a real challenge for dyslexic learners. Thus, if spelling is used as a criterion, the student will have a distinct disadvantage if restrained from using an appropriate tool to aid in correct spelling.

SUGGESTIONS FOR COLLEGE FACULTY INTERESTED IN ASSISTING STUDENTS WITH LEARNING DIFFICULTIES

1. Announce your willingness to help students who have learning difficulties. Have them identify themselves via written message or make an appointment to discuss their specialized learning needs.

2. Outline the academic performance expectations at the beginning of the course.

3. Provide students with a detailed course syllabus.

4. Start each lecture with an outline of material to be covered. If this isn't possible, visually list the major objectives that will be the focus of the lecture.

5. Summarize the key points at the conclusion of the class.

6. Give directions in specific, sequential steps. Numbering each step is helpful.

7. Present information in visual as well as audible form.

8. Recognize that students who have specific language disabilities may not be able to take notes as quickly as other students. Allow the student to use a notetaker.

9. Allow students to tape-record the lecture if so desired.

10. Let students choose their best seating location.

11. Permit students to use aids for spelling.

12. Provide a study guide for examinations well in advance of the test date.

13. Permit students to write on the examination booklet. Identifying the key words in a question or visually eliminating some words or choices is beneficial.

14. Make provisions for examinations to be in larger print.

15. Allow students extra time on major projects and examinations.

16. View students with learning difficulties as competent and capable students with unique learning approaches.

Enrichment Activities

1. Identify your learning strengths and appraise them in relationship to your academic requirements.

2. Review the suggestions for college faculty interested in assisting students with learning difficulties. Using elements of critical thinking, specify your reasons for supporting or not supporting these suggestions.

3. If you have a learning difficulty, how have you been helped/hindered by college personnel?

4. Many capable college students have learning difficulties, either documented or undocumented. Describe your difficulty or those you know about and discuss how they could be managed.

5. What accommodations would you like to be available to *all* students?

6. Invite personnel from the Student Support Center to share information about learning difficulties, resources, and legal ramifications for colleges.

20

Suggestions for Success

The following suggestions were gleaned from experiences of students and teachers throughout the United States. Some are personal reflections, while others are statements to be contemplated. Each is considered good advice for any person pursuing academic endeavors.

1. Keep your sense of humor.
2. Ask questions until you understand.
3. Study for long-term memory.
4. Avoid too much caffeine.
5. Get a tutor before it's too late.
6. Review your notes right after class.
7. Use flash cards to help you memorize information.
8. Exercise on a daily basis.
9. Find a quiet place to study.
10. Do more than is required.
11. Use an electronic organizer.
12. Establish a routine.
13. Get plenty of sleep.

14. Study with a partner.

15. Take all the time you can for a test.

16. Ask professors to give a test study guide.

17. Get a head start on your reading.

18. Fight the odds.

19. Give yourself rewards.

20. Start research papers early.

21. Take hard classes in the summer.

22. Parent yourself.

23. Eat healthily.

24. Trick your mind into thinking you like something even if you don't.

25. Go to summer school.

26. Read all your assignments.

27. Take quality notes.

28. Burn an assignment into your brain. Live it, breathe it, think it; let it become a part of you.

29. Divide large projects into small steps.

30. Read information on university bulletin boards.

31. Spend lots of time studying. It works!

32. Study smart.

33. Be patient.

34. Keep up with your homework.

35. Make lots of friends.

36. Develop a good attitude.

37. Be pleasant and polite.

38. Work hard. College can sneak up on you.

39. Get work experience.

40. Take aptitude and interest tests.

41. Do internships.

42. Be happy.

43. Be sure your professors know you by name.

44. Be persistent.

45. Balance work with recreation and pleasure.

46. Approach each semester as a fresh beginning.

47. Travel and get a global perspective.
48. Attend all classes.
49. Demonstrate leadership skills.
50. Avoid complaining.
51. Resist the easy way out.
52. Keep things in proper perspective.
53. Learn from everyone.
54. Use the resources of the university.
55. Read the university newspaper.
56. Recognize your limitations.
57. Learn how the system works.
58. Understand that the university is not against you.
59. Try and fail, but never fail to try.
60. Be resourceful.
61. Explore all the available avenues.
62. Expand your horizons.
63. Get good grades.
64. Pretend the professor gives daily quizzes.
65. Remember that learning is a process.
66. Face your anxieties.
67. Avoid procrastination.
68. Know your learning styles.
69. See it! Say it! Do it!
70. Use multisensory learning strategies.
71. Use the library.
72. Resolve past hurts. They interfere with learning.
73. Find a listening friend.
74. Do your best; always give more than the rest.
75. Study even if you don't have specific homework.
76. Being too social can be the death of good grades.
77. Remember that you're attending college to get an education.
78. Choose extracurricular activities that will enhance your career.
79. Learn how to use technology.
80. Survive your freshman year.

"Clayborn! This is indeed a surprise!

81. Practice designing objective examinations.
82. Make up essay questions. Write the answers.
83. Take tests backwards.
84. Find a way that works for you and stick to it.
85. Get to know your professors.
86. Sit where the professor will see you.
87. Demonstrate confidence.
88. Overlearn.
89. Learn from those who do well.

90. Emulate good role models.

91. Attend university events and seminars.

92. Study just before going to bed.

93. Get to know other students in your classes.

94. Study as if you are the professor and will be giving the lecture.

95. Demonstrate good listening skills.

96. Keep track of your grades.

97. Perform community service.

98. Show appreciation.

99. Pray for wisdom.

100. Recognize the extraordinary nature of the college experience. Never again will you be in a little society as unique in composition and purpose. College is a microcosm of life. It is an opportunity to build a foundation for living that will stand the test of time.

Graduation!

 ongratulations!
You have met all the requirements for graduation!

1. Shout hallelujah!
2. Tell everyone you know!
3. Thank your professors!
4. Pick up your cap and gown!
5. Sell your books!
6. Call home!
7. Get a job!
8. Pay back loans!
9. Clean your room!
10. Be proud! You did it!

References

Aaron, P. G., and Catherine Baker. (1991). *Reading disabilities in college and high school: Diagnosis and management.* Parkton, MD: York Press.

Armstrong, William H. (1995). *Study is hard work,* 2nd ed. Boston: David R. Godine.

Arnot, Robert. (2000). *The biology of success.* Boston: Little, Brown.

Ayto, John. (1990). *Dictionary of word origins.* New York: Arcade Publishing.

Beaumont, J. Graham. (1989). *Brain power.* New York: Harper and Row.

Berts, Marjorie E., and Margaret Gisler. (1999). *How to prepare for college,* 2nd ed. Chicago: Contemporary Publishing Group.

Bickerhoff, Loring C., Stan F. Shaw, and Joan M. McGuire. (1993). *Promoting postsecondary education for students with learning disabilities.* Austin, TX: PRO-ED.

Bliss, Edwin. (1976). *Getting things done.* New York: Bantam Books.

Bourne, Edmund. (1998). *Healing fear.* Oakland, CA: New Harbinger Publications.

Bruno, Frank J. (2001). *Going back to school: College survival strategies for adult students.* Lawrenceville, NJ: Thomson Peterson's.

Carlson, Neil R. (1996). *Psychology: The science of behavior,* 5th ed. Boston: Allyn & Bacon.

Carnegie, Dale. (1936). *How to win friends and influence people.* New York: Simon and Schuster.

Carper, Jean. (2000). *Your miracle brain.* New York: HarperCollins.

Central Michigan University. (2000). 2000–2001 *Bulletin,* Vol. 106, No. 1. Mt. Pleasant, MI.

Comeauz, Patricia, *ed.* (2005). *Assessing online learning.* Bolton, MA: Anker Publishing Company.

Devine, Thomas G. (1987). *Teaching study skills: A guide for teachers.* Boston: Allyn & Bacon.

Dobkin, Rachel, and Shana Sippy. (1995). *The college woman's handbook*. New York: Workman Publishers.

Dunn, Rita, and Kenneth Dunn. (1993). *Teaching students to read through their individual learning style*. Boston: Allyn & Bacon.

Ehrlich, Ida. (1988). *Instant vocabulary*. New York: Pocket Books.

Ellis, David B. (2006). *Becoming a master student*, 11th ed. Boston: Houghton Mifflin.

Evans, Eric T. (1998). *The art of academic success*. Los Angeles: Nova Press.

Flippo, Rona F., and David D. Caverly, eds. (1991). *Teaching reading and study strategies at the college level*. Newark: International Reading Association.

Fry, Ron. (1999). *The great big book of how to study*. Clifton Park, NY: Thomson Delmar Learning.

Grayson, Paul A., and Philip W. Meilman. (1999). *Beating the college blues*, 2nd ed. New York: Checkmark Books.

Hamachek, Alice L. (1989). Study strategies for the secondary student: Enhancing memory. *Michigan Reading Journal* 22:22–26.

Hamachek, Alice L. (1990). *Interactive reading-teaching model for secondary reading: A new direction for the future*. Grand Rapids: Michigan Reading Association.

Hamachek, Alice L., and Frank A. Stancato. (1990). The interactive nature and reciprocal effects of cognitive and affective learning. *Education* 3(1): 77–81.

Holkeboer, Robert. (1993). *Right from the start: Managing your way to college success*. Belmont, CA: Wadsworth.

Iaccoca, Lee. (1986). *Iacocca: An autobiography*. New York: Bantam.

Jensen, Eric. (2003). *Student success secrets*. Hauppauge, NY: Barron's.

Kinneavy, James L., and John E. Warriner. (2000). *Elements of writing: Fifth Course*. Orlando, FL: Holt, Rinehart and Winston.

Kuh, George D., *et al*. (2005). *Student success in college: Creating conditions that matter*. San Francisco: Jossey-Bass.

Losyk, Bob. (2005). *Get a grip: Overcoming stress and thriving in the workplace*. Hoboken, NJ: John Wiley & Sons.

Lunsford, Andrea, and Robert Conners. (1989). *The St. Martin's handbook*. New York: St. Martin's Press.

Mather, Peter, and Rita McCarthy. (2005). *The art of critical reading: Brushing up on your reading, thinking, and study skills*. Boston: McGraw-Hill.

Miller, George. (1956). The magical number seven: Plus or minus two. *Psychological Review* 63:81–97.

Morgenstern, Julie. (2004). *Organizing from the inside out,* 2nd ed. New York: Henry Holt and Company.

Nemko, Marty. (1999). *You're gonna love this college guide.* New York: Barron's Educational Series.

Nichols, Ralph G. (1960). *The supervisor's notebook,* Vol. 22, No. 1. New York: Scott, Foresman and Company.

Nosich, Gerald M. (2001). *Learning to think things through: A guide to critical thinking across the curriculum.* Upper Saddle River, NJ: Prentice Hall.

Olney, Claude W. (1988). *Where there's a will there's an A.* Paoli, PA: Chesterbrook Educational Publishers.

Ornstein, Robert, and Richard F. Thompson. (1984). *The amazing brain.* Boston: Houghton Mifflin.

Paul, Richard, and Linda Elder. (2001). *Critical thinking: Tools for taking charge of your learning and your life.* Upper Saddle River, NJ: Prentice Hall.

Petrie, Trent, and Eric Denson. (1999). *A student athlete's guide to college success.* Belmont, CA: Wadsworth Publishing Company.

Rich, Jason. (1993). *The everything college survival book.* Holbrook, MA: Adams Media Corporation.

Robinson, Adam. (1993). *What smart students know.* New York: Three Rivers Press.

Robinson, Francis P. (1941). *Effective study.* New York: Harper and Row.

Scheiber, Barbara, and Jeanne Talpers. (1987). *Unlocking potential.* Bethesda, MD: Adler and Adler, Publishers.

Sebrankek, Patrick, Vern Meyer, and Dave Kemper. (1992). *Writer's Inc.* Burlington, WI: Write Source Educational Publishing House.

Seligman, Martin. (1990). *Learned optimism.* New York: Pocket Books.

Shafir, Rebecca Z. (2000). *The zen of listening.* Wheaton, IL: Quest Books.

Shepherd, James F. (1981). *RSVP The Houghton Mifflin reading, studying and vocabulary program.* Boston: Houghton Mifflin.

Shepherd, James F. (1987). *College vocabulary skills.* Boston: Houghton Mifflin.

Silver, Theodore. (1992). *The Princeton review: Study smart.* New York: Random House.

Sprenger, Merilee. (2003). *Differentiation through learning styles and memory.* Thousand Oaks, CA: Corwin Press.

Stine, Jean Marie. (1997). *Double your brain power*. Englewood Cliffs, NJ: Prentice Hall.

Teele, Sue. (2004). *Overcoming barricades to reading: A multiple intelligences approach*. Thousand Oaks, CA: Corwin Press.

Ziglar, Zig. (2000). *See you at the top*, 2nd rev. ed. Gretna, LA: Pelican Publishing Company.

Index